The Principles of New Thought

The Principles of New Thought

Tracing Spiritual Truth
From the Source to the Soul

BY

APRIL MONCRIEFF

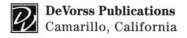
DeVorss Publications
Camarillo, California

THE PRINCIPLES OF NEW THOUGHT
Copyright ©2013
by April Moncrieff

ISBN: 9780875168739
First Printing, 2013

DeVorss & Company, Publisher
P.O. Box 1389
Camarillo CA 93011-1389
www.devorss.com

Printed in the United States of America

Library of Congress Cataloging-in-Publication Data

Moncrieff, April.
The principles of new thought : tracing spiritual truth from the source to the soul / by
April Moncrieff.
    pages cm
  Includes bibliographical references.
  ISBN 978-0-87516-873-9 (pbk. : alk. paper)
1. New Thought.
2. Christianity and other religions--New Thought.
3. New Thought--Relations--Christianity. I. Title.
  BF639.M6645 2013
  299'.93--dc23

                                                                2013008537

ACKNOWLEDGEMENTS

This book is lovingly dedicated to my parents

Reverend Malcolm Alexander Moncrieff

and

Virginia Freeman Moncrieff

The first and greatest of my spiritual teachers

and

to all of the souls who have touched my life

in a special way and enriched my spiritual journey

Table of Contents

The religion of the future will be a cosmic religion. It will have to transcend a personal God and avoid dogma and theology. Encompassing both the natural and the spiritual, it will have to be based on a religious sense arising from the experience of all things, natural and spiritual, considered as a meaningful unity.

— ALBERT EINSTEIN

I do dimly perceive that whilst everything around me is ever-changing, ever-dying, there is, underlying all that change, a living power that is changeless, that holds all together, that creates, dissolves, and recreates. That informing power or spirit is God...I see it as purely benevolent, for I can see that in the midst of death, life persists; in the midst of untruth, truth persists. Hence I gather that God is life, truth and light. He is love. He is the supreme good. But He is no God who merely satisfies the intellect, if he ever does. God to be God, must rule the heart and transform it.

— MAHATMA GANDHI, from a 1932 recording

Within man is the soul of the whole; the wise silence; the universal beauty, to which every part and particle is equally related; the eternal ONE. And this deep power in which we exist and whose beatitude is all accessible to us, is not only self-sufficing and perfect in every hour, but the act of seeing and the thing seen, the seer and the spectacle, the subject and the object, are one. We see the world piece by piece, as the sun, the moon, the animal, the tree; but the whole of which these are the shining parts, is the soul.

Thus revering the soul, and learning, as the ancients said, that "its beauty is immense," man will come to see that the world is the perennial miracle which the soul worketh, and be less astonished at particular wonders; he will learn that there is no profane history; that all history is sacred; that the universe is represented in an atom, in a moment of time. He will weave no longer a spotted life of shreds and patches, but he will live with a divine unity. He will cease from what is false and frivolous in his own life and be content with all places and any service he can render. He will calmly front the morrow in the negligency of that trust which carries God with it and so hath already the whole future in the bottom of the heart.

— RALPH WALDO EMERSON, essay on The Oversoul

What is New Thought?

Behold, I maketh all things new.
— Jesus Christ

The New Thought is the Christ thought made new by being
applied and proved in every day affairs.
— from the INTA Bulletin, December 15, 1916

Hitherto we have taken forms and conditions as the starting point
of our thought and inferred that they are the causes of mental
states; now we have learnt that the true order of the creative
process is exactly the reverse, and that thought and feeling are
the causes, and forms and conditions the effects. When we have
learnt this lesson we have grasped the foundation principle on
which individual specialization of the generic law of the creative
process becomes a practical possibility.

New Thought, then, is not the name of a particular sect, but is
the essential factor by which our own future development is
to be carried on; and its essence consists in seeing the relation
of things in a New Order. Hitherto we have inverted the true
order of cause and effect; now by carefully considering the true

nature of the Principle of Causation in itself — *causa causans as* distinguished from *causa causata* — we return to the true order and adopt a new method of thinking in accordance with it.

In themselves, this order and this method of thinking are not new. They are older than the foundation of the world, for they are those of the Creative Spirit itself; and all through the ages this teaching has been handed down through various forms, the true meaning of which has been perceived only by a few in each generation. But as the light breaks in upon any individual it is a new light to him, and so to each one in succession it becomes the New Thought. And when anyone reaches it he finds himself in a New Order.

— THOMAS TROWARD, *The Dore Lectures on Mental Science*

New Thought and The Bible

A deeply interesting subject to the student of the New Thought movement is to trace how deeply its teaching is endorsed by the teaching of the Bible…I have no hesitation in saying that the existence of a marked correspondence between its teaching and that of the New Thought cannot but be a source of strength and encouragement to any of us who have been accustomed in the past to look to the old and hallowed book as a source of Divine wisdom. We shall find that the clearer light will make the rough places smooth and the dim places luminous and that of the treasures hidden in the ancient volume the half has not been told us.

— THOMAS TROWARD, *The Hidden Power*

The Bible is not like any other book; it is the spiritual vortex through which power pours from heaven to earth, and the reason most people derive comparatively little profit from its study is that they lack the spiritual key.

— EMMET FOX, *Power through Constructive Thinking*

The Bible is not a book outside of [us]; it is not a series of events which took place thousands of years ago. Scripture is the unfolding of characters and happenings or movements that are taking place within [us] – right this moment. Every Biblical experience can be found in [our] consciousness at some time or other. [We], therefore, embody within [ourselves] every Bible of the world, every philosophy, character and story.

— JOEL GOLDSMITH, *The Spiritual Interpretation of Scripture*

The Bible is a very wonderful book...it is a deep exposition of mental laws and it is also a treatise on the true physiological estate of the body. It shows that the human organism is mind in action, rather than an aggregation of purely material functions. But above all, the Bible explains the spiritual character of man, and the laws governing his relation to God.

— CHARLES FILLMORE, *Christian Healing*

The Bibles of the world tell of two powers, of good and of evil — but that is because Scripture should not be interpreted merely as historical documents but as the spiritually revealed Truth of inspired sages and seers. In this light there is but one Presence, one Power — and I AM that.

— JOEL GOLDSMITH, *The Spiritual Interpretation of Scripture*

Jesus…lived in a world of spiritual realization far beyond that of which the average man has any understanding…so the full meaning of his sayings can never be clear to us until we have attained a consciousness equal to his. But in the record of his sayings there is much which bears witness to our own [New Thought] belief, and no doubt could we penetrate the meaning of his teaching, we should have a perfect explanation of our own philosophy.

— ERNEST HOLMES, *The Science of Mind*

Introduction

Churchianity, by substituting creed for Christ and dogma
instead of the divine facts of being, has stripped Love of her
royal robes and has left her standing an unheeded
beggar in the universe of God.

— Rev. W. John Murray

All of the world's great religions have sacred writings that
are considered to be the definitive and infallible guide to their
spiritual beliefs and practices. For mainstream Christians, in
particular, the collected scriptures that comprise the Holy Bible
are deemed the direct and final word of God and the supreme
authority in matters pertaining to human conduct. Each word
inscribed within its pages is regarded as a literal account of the
historical events of several thousand years ago and the only
source of truth about God and creation. Dissenters challenge
the veracity and authority of the Bible at their peril.

In the enlightened philosophy of New Thought, however,
where the metaphysical or non-literal interpretation of the
Christian Bible is sought, we discern a deeper significance to all

of the characters, places and events described within its pages. In prayerful contemplation as we read, the spiritual Truth within the words is revealed, Truth that is at once illumined and inspired, and soundly practical in its relevance to daily life. Our recognition of the Truth contained within the teachings of the Bible, when applied faithfully and systematically to the problems at hand, sets us free from confusion, doubt and fear and we begin to live, as Thoreau claimed in *Walden*, "with the license of a higher order of beings."

In this book, some of the key tenets of orthodox Christianity will be enumerated. Then we will examine these dogmas and beliefs with the greater understanding afforded by spiritual revelation. With the awareness that "spiritual things must be spiritually discerned", specific verses and passages from the Bible will be cited and interpreted in the light of the New Thought teachings. Well-known metaphysical authors' insights will be offered as corroboration. The teachings and demonstration of Jesus Christ, in particular, will be elucidated in the context of New Thought principles, with special attention to the spiritual laws underlying the regeneration of the physical body.

The Principles of New Thought

CHAPTER 1

The Nature of God

I AM God and there is none else (Isa. 45:22).

God is Love and there is nothing in existence but
God and His self-expression.
— EMMET FOX, treatment on *Divine Love*

In the beginning was the Word and the Word was
with God and the Word was God (Jn.1:1).

So let us begin at the beginning!

Many of the world's sacred scriptures that have come down
to us through the millennia tell of two distinct and irreconcilable
powers, one good, the other evil. For each belief in an all-loving
benevolent Deity there is the belief in an equal but opposing
force that seeks at every turn to thwart the good intentions of a
loving Creator. In many representations of the Supreme Being
God Himself is believed to be dualistic in nature, as capable of
destruction as He is of creation. Nowhere is this dichotomy
more evident than in the doctrines of mainstream Christianity

and the collection of writings that comprise its primary source, the Christian Bible.

In the books of the Old Testament and the main denominations of Christianity God is portrayed as a venerable patriarchal figure ruling His Creation from a throne located somewhere "up there" in a realm called Heaven. This anthropomorphic vision of the Creator of the Universe has been supported down through the centuries by depictions of God in literature, music and great works of art such as Michelangelo's Sistine Chapel masterpiece *The Creation of Adam,* as an austere larger-than-life Being, usually sporting a long white beard. Many sincere churchgoers still subscribe to this view of the Supreme Being.

In his essay on *The Seven Main Aspects of God,* beloved metaphysical author, minister and teacher, Emmet Fox, writes that in his experience "even today, the majority of people, in their hearts, do think of God as…a magnified man…a very good man, an extraordinarily wise man, a man of infinite powers, but still a man" (AYL, p.119). In this conception of God as man-on-a-superhuman-scale, Christians have ascribed to God many of the same qualities humankind possesses, in particular, as we have said, a twofold nature.

In this vision of the Supreme Being as the very essence of *duality,* invested in equal measure with both benevolent and destructive impulses, His conflicting intentions are directed most often toward His greatest creation, *man.* An austere Father-figure, God is not only somewhat unresponsive to His most celebrated creation, humankind, He is upon occasion punitive, particularly if it is determined that man has been disobedient. Because God acts randomly rather than according to law, He is seen as playing favorites. Therefore, like an autocratic ruler, He must be endlessly placated by His subjects. Elaborate prayers and religious rituals are devised through which man attempts to appease God and assure himself of Divine favor. This characterization of God as the anthropomorphized extension of humankind endowed with equal propensities toward good and evil has occurred because "scripture has been accepted from the standpoint of literal translation instead of being read in the light of spiritual inspiration" (SIOS).

The philosophy of New Thought, often referred to as *metaphysical Christianity* because we look *beyond* the literal historical account of Creation and the conception of the Supreme Being as a glorified version of man, presents a more mature understanding of the nature of God. We move, as Dr. Fox puts it, "beyond this infantile stage to the truth" (P.120). We transcend the depiction of God as an anthropomorphic figure — man on a superhuman scale – and recognize God as Spirit, Omnipresent, First Cause, without beginning and end, permeating all space and what we experience as time. Ernest Holmes, founder of the Religious Science movement (now known as Centers for Spiritual Living, or CSL) and author of the comprehensive volume *The Science of Mind,* characterizes God as "the Absolute, the Unconditioned, the One and Only Spirit, or Creative Energy which is the cause of all visible things" (SOM, P.596).

Emmet Fox reminds us, too, that since God is Infinite Being we cannot define Him, because that would be to limit Him. We can, however, in our search to understand the true nature of God, gain "an excellent working knowledge of Him by considering different aspects of His nature" (P.121). Dr. Fox goes on to enumerate seven main aspects or attributes of God which he lists as Life, Truth, Love, Intelligence, Soul, Spirit and Principle. By pondering these exalted qualities in turn, we become acquainted with the nature of God and by inference, of our own nature as sons and daughters of the Most High (Ps.82:6), made in His image and likeness (Gen.1:26).

In the New Thought view, then, we deny the existence of a dual-natured Deity. We believe that God is not two, but One, and assert that recognizing the indivisible nature of God is the key to understanding who WE, as the offspring of God, are. The great 20th century metaphysician Joel Goldsmith writes in *Practicing the Presence:*

> How can God be held responsible for [the evils of accidents, disasters, and sickness] in the light of the message of the Master, which was the healing of the sick, the raising of the dead, the feeding of the hungry, and the overcoming of every kind of disaster…If God tolerates these evils or is a human parent teaching us a lesson, how can we rise above them and return to the Father's house? From the very beginning of … spiritual study, we…learn that God is the one power, the all-power, and not only the all-power, but the all-good power. The Master said, "I am not come to destroy but to fulfill" (p.38).

As we look beneath the surface text, we find Biblical support for our enlightened understanding of the nature of God as Oneness, indivisible perfect Good, throughout its pages. Even in the Old Testament, where God is often represented as embodying both positive and negative attributes, we find clear statements about the nature of God as ONE entity, One Being, One Presence, One Power, One Principle, and that Principle is pure and Absolute Good. "I am the Lord and there is none else;

there is no God beside me," we read in Isaiah (45:5), and in Exodus we find this affirmation of the indissoluble Unity of Being in the magnificent words uttered to Moses from the burning bush: "I AM that I AM" (Exo.3:14). As Pure and Absolute Good, Indivisible, the Power that knows Itself, God has no cognizance of anything BUT good. So we can say with the author of Habbakuk who recognized the great Truth of God as Perfect Good: "Thou art of purer eyes than to behold … iniquity" (Hab.1:13).

Metaphysicians have always recognized God as the only Power and the nature of God as Absolute Good. Since we know that there *is* only One Presence, One Power, One Mind and One Law operative in the Universe, God the Good, Omnipotent, all that appears to be evil, or a power at work that would oppose God, is illusion, the incomplete, imperfect and distorted assessment of the five human senses. Dr. Fox expresses the nature of God as One Perfect Indivisible entity in his meditation entitled "The Presence," excerpted here:

> God is the only Real Presence. All the rest is but shadow. God is perfect good and God is the Cause only of Perfect Good. God never sends sickness, trouble, accident, temptation, nor death itself. We bring them upon ourselves by our own wrong thinking. God, good, can cause only Good. "The same fountain cannot send forth both sweet and bitter water" (James 3:11).

Thus, the vengefulness often attributed to God in certain parts of the Bible and incorporated into the doctrines of mainstream Christianity, must in fact, have a deeper meaning. In a splendid insight, Joel Goldsmith explains the apparent vindictiveness of God as *the destruction of error in consciousness*, the dissolution of the belief in the validity of error — any power or presence apart from the One — in whatever guise it may present itself. In Truth there is no enemy to be fought with or destroyed, only the recognition of error for what it is, a "mirage" or nothingness, needing only to be "recognized as such to reveal its impotence" (SIS, P.75).

Another belief prevalent among mainstream Christians is that God is essentially separate from His creation and for the most part detached from human affairs and concerns. In the Old Testament, especially, we find this characterization of an external Deity, a God who having once created man, is usually distant from him thereafter and localized to a far-off celestial region called Heaven, which, as we said, is thought of as being somewhere in the sky. The Deity intervenes randomly and sporadically in human affairs but remains generally removed from man and inaccessible to him.

We metaphysicians, on the other hand, affirm the Omnipresence of God. Unlike Christian fundamentalists, we do not believe that God is remote, unapproachable, and indifferent to our needs. Rather, we assert that God is Omnipresent, and that as such He is not only transcendent, but im*man*ent (indwelling *us*). Far from being confined to the heavenly spheres, God as Spirit is everywhere equally present and permeates all time and space. He is, therefore, immediately accessible at all times. We declare, however, that while God as Omnipresence fills all space, our point of contact with Omniscient Being is always *within*.

Although a superficial reading of the Old Testament might lead us to subscribe to the belief that God is a remote Deity, as we delve more deeply into the Bible, we find repeated assurances that God is not a distant entity, confined to an intangible realm somewhere in the far-off celestial regions. Rather, He is intimately present with us and within us at all times as the Living Presence, the Eternal Law of our own Being. Throughout the Scriptures we find support for the New Thought teaching of the instantaneous and constant availability of God. In the beautiful words of the Psalms and the Acts of the Apostles, we read these comforting assurances:

> Closer is he than breathing, and nearer than hands and feet. God (is) a very present help in trouble (Ps.46:1).

> In him we live and move and have our being (Acts 17:28).

Instead of the insecurity that fundamentalist Christians may experience by believing God to be far away and perhaps unmoved by their plight, we are uplifted by the assurance of the steadfast Love of our Creator, and draw strength as we gain a deeper sense of the Truth that "underneath *are* the everlasting arms" (Deut.33:27). We take comfort from the certain knowledge that God has not only created us, but that He sustains us from moment to moment. As we realize our intimate relationship with the Divinity, we can claim with the Apostle John "Greater is He that is in me than he [any condition] that is in the world" (1 Jn.4:4).

Because we *do* know the Truth that we live and move and have our Being in the One Presence, we declare that we are fully equipped on the spiritual level to meet and handle any challenge that comes our way. We are victorious in any adverse circumstance simply by consciously knowing and *identifying with* the tremendous spiritual resources we have at our command right within our own being. This means, however, that we must intentionally, and with the expectation of good results, take a bold stand against fear and *for* the outcome we desire to see manifest. One Truth statement that is very useful in helping us feel empowered when negative appearances attempt to claim our allegiance is "None of these things moves me" (ACTS 20:24).

Former Unity minister and author Mary Kupferle offers these uplifting words:

> Every time you arise, each time you take this stand of Christ-like dominion, blessings will follow. You will realize a great calm in your mind and heart concerning all false appearances each time you let God work in and through you to bring forth good. You will find all demoniac trials hold nothing but gain and promise, that all feverish conditions promise nothing but purity and refreshment for the awakening of new spiritual values and material enrichment (GNF, P.58).

A third significant way in which our New Thought view of the nature of God differs markedly from that of our fundamentalist friends is this: Mainstream "believers" would convince us that the Supreme Being is unpredictable, inconsistent or random in Its workings, dispensing favors to some, while doling out punishments to others. Since we know the nature of God to be Absolute Good we realize, therefore, that God cannot violate Its own nature by displaying such human qualities as negative behavior or capricious actions. In other words, God does not play favorites! This is a Universe of order, harmony, and balance, based upon eternal Spiritual laws we are just beginning to discover and tap into, and these principles are encoded within the very cells and atoms of our being. Through turning within in moments of quiet prayer and meditation we become aware of these laws and are guided to apply them.

We discover teachings on the nature of God as Universal Law throughout the Bible (AYL, p. 119). In the New Testament, we find the metaphysical recognition of God as impersonal Law implicit in such statements as Peter's "God is no respecter of persons" (ACTS 10:34) and Jesus' words from the Sermon on the Mount: "Your Father...sendeth rain on the just *and* on the unjust" (MATT.5:45). Even as early as the Old Testament Book of Jeremiah we find allusions to the great laws that govern our being:

> I will put my law in their inward parts and I will write it
> in their heart (JER.31:33).

In New Thought we understand the word 'heart' to refer to the deeper levels of one's being, wherein Divinity, as Subjective Intelligence, resides. It is here that we discover the Universal Laws upon which Creation rests, the Principles that form the very foundation of our identity as the offspring of and co-creators with, God, eternal principles that support, prosper and bless us as we learn to cooperate consciously and intentionally with them.

Uplifted and strengthened by our *experiential* understanding that God as unfailing Principle is always near, a "very present help in trouble", the eternal fount of blessings poured forth ceaselessly from the inexhaustible Source of perfect Good, we followers of New Thought derive a deep and unshakable sense of security that is not threatened by the exigencies of life. We can claim with Job that even in the midst of every conceivable trial:

> I *know* my redeemer liveth (JOB 19:25).

CHAPTER 2

The Trinity of Being

The trinity of being appears to run through
all nature and all life.
— ERNEST HOLMES, *The Science of Mind*

The doctrine of the Trinity is often a stumbling block,
because we find it difficult to understand how three
persons can be one. Three persons cannot be one, and
theology will always be a mystery until theologians become
metaphysicians.
— CHARLES FILLMORE, *The Revealing Word*

The principal aspects of God are Life, Truth, and Love.
These are the great Trinity in which Mind expresses Itself.
— EMMET FOX, *Power through Constructive Thinking*

Although Christianity is considered a monotheistic religion
— all Christians claim to believe in One God – the doctrine
of God as three literal persons is one of the cardinal tenets of
orthodox Christianity. For mainstream believers the Holy
Trinity comprises first God, the Father (often depicted, as

noted previously, as the white-bearded patriarchal Creator of Renaissance art); next, the Son, Jesus Christ, the immaculately conceived sole offspring of the Heavenly Father, and third, the Holy Spirit, an amorphous entity that intervenes from time to time in human affairs. But as Charles Fillmore, co-founder of the Unity movement, points out in the opening quotation from *The Revealing Word*, accepting the doctrine of the Trinity at face value presents a problem to our understanding.

As we begin to study metaphysical truth, we learn that the notion of a threefold Deity embraces far more than the limited concept described above. "Turn it as we will," Ernest Holmes writes in his great textbook, throughout all of existence "we are confronted with the necessity of the trinity of being" (p.80) and recognize the theme of 'three' operating throughout the manifest plane. We describe physical objects in terms of their length, width and height. Physicians categorize body types as ectomorph, mesomorph and endomorph; practitioners of ayurveda, the traditional medical practice of India, separate body types into vata, kapha, and pitta. Students of the American political system learn from the outset that the government of the United States is comprised of three main branches – executive, legislative and judicial, incorporated into a threefold foundational structure of checks and balances.

The notion of trinity is evident in psychology and mythology, as well. Freudian psychoanalysts compartmentalize the human psyche into three areas: the conscious, the unconscious and the *id*. The mythology of ancient Greece and Rome is peopled with numerous triplet beings: among them, the three Fates, the three Furies, the three snake-haired Gorgon sisters, and even Cerberus, the three-head hound who guarded the gates to the Underworld.

We discern that the threefold nature of existence pervades every level of thought and expression on the manifest plane and extends even to the concepts of God depicted in the world's cultural and spiritual traditions. Indeed, the trinitarian character of Being figures prominently in the world's great religions, even permeating concepts of divinity in the great cultures and religions that pre-date Christianity. H. P. Blavatsky in *Isis Unveiled* (pp. 45,46), reveals that the Trinity Dogma originated from Babylon:

> We find it northeast of the Indus; and tracing it to Asia Minor and Europe, recognize it among every people who had anything like an established religion. It was taught in the oldest Chaldaean, Egyptian, and Mithraitic schools. The Chaldaean Sun-god, Mithra, was called 'Triple,' and the trinitarian idea of the Chaldaeans was a doctrine of the Akkadians, who themselves belonged to a race which was the first to conceive a metaphysical trinity.

And James Hastings writes in the *Encyclopedia of Religion and Ethics:*

> In Indian religion, e.g., we meet with the trinitarian group of Brahma, Shiva, and Vishnu; and in Egyptian religion with the trinitarian group of Osiris, Isis, and Horus. . .Nor is it only in historical religions that we find God viewed as a Trinity. One recalls in particular the Neo-Platonic views of the Supreme or Ultimate Reality, which is triadically represented.

Thus, it is no surprise that the archetypal notion of a trinity of Being found its way into Christian theology. While there is no specific reference to a Holy Trinity, as such, in either the Old or New Testament and it is not explicitly taught by Jesus as a doctrine, subliminal awareness of the triple-phased nature of existence was incorporated into Christian dogma and Christians intuitively depict the Godhead in a trinitarian aspect.

Metaphysicians discern, however, that the Christian trinity of Father, Son, and Holy Spirit is a *symbolic representation of the triune nature of Being Itself* and therefore of our own threefold nature composed of spirit, mind, and body. With the deeper understanding of New Thought, we view the Christian trinity of Father, Son, and Holy Spirit, as designations for the three phases of Mind: Mind, Idea, and Expression. In the Unity teachings, for example, the Father or First Person of the Trinity, represents Divine Mind; the Son or offspring of Divine Mind of course represents the Divine Idea, and the Holy Spirit is regarded as Divine Mind in Expression.

Ernest Holmes of Religious Science (CSL) states that "Man is a threefold principle of life and action; he is spirit, soul, and body" (P.476). He delineates the Trinity this way: "There is the Thing (Absolute Intelligence), the way It works (Absolute Law) and what It does (the results, or manifestation)" (SOM, P.80). He goes on to say:

> We have every reason to postulate a threefold nature of the Universal being: which we shall call Spirit, Soul, and Body. We shall think of Spirit as the great Actor, Soul as the medium of Its action, and Body the result of Its action. We shall think of Spirit as the only Conscious Actor – the Power that knows Itself. We shall think of Soul as a blind Force, obeying the will of Spirit; and we shall think of Body as the effect of Spirit, working through Law to produce form (SOM, P. 129).

This sequence plays out throughout all of Creation, including humankind. Holmes states:

> Man re-enacts the Divine Nature on all three planes. He is self-knowing in his conscious mind, creative through his subconscious reactions, and he has a body (SOM, P.176).

While in our spiritual nature we are multi-dimensional beings expressing simultaneously in many different dimensionalities and planes of consciousness, the most familiar sense of self we possess at present is of course our identity as three-dimensional creatures in a three-dimensional world. At this level, we are made up of three primary energy fields – mental, emotional and physical. Tony Stubbs writes in his enlightening little manual titled *An Ascension Handbook*, each with our own unique "blend of frequencies and relative amplitudes" that "define us as a body and a personality" (P. 46). Thus, in our individuality of expression on the manifest plane, each of us personifies the Trinity of Being.

In her excellent nine-cd series entitled *Entering the Castle,* spiritual teacher and author Caroline Myss, shares 15th century Catholic mystic Saint Theresa of Avila's insight into the "true meaning of the [Christian] Trinity." Like all those in whom the spiritual faculty of discernment is awakened, Myss tells us, Theresa recognized that the Trinity "had nothing to do with a Father, a Son, and a Holy Spirit", that these figures are in fact universal archetypes that together comprise a "cosmic template of power, truth, and knowledge."

While the Trinity is not explicitly mentioned in the Bible nor taught directly by Jesus, as we noted, the threefold character of Being permeates the great text in subtle ways that are readily perceived by New Thought students. A striking example of the trinity in evidence appears in the Old Testament saga of the Israelites held in bondage in Egypt and ultimately set free, recounted at great length in the book of Exodus and interpreted metaphysically by Joel Goldsmith. An in-depth study of these chapters reveals that the conditions experienced by the Israelites correspond to three distinct phases of consciousness that all of humanity moves through in the course of its spiritual unfoldment. The story of the Israelites in Egypt and their journey through trials and challenges to ultimate freedom and fulfillment is a marvelous summation of our *individual* spiritual odyssey and a brilliant illustration of the metaphysical significance of the Holy Trinity.

In the first stage, the Israelites are held in bondage in Egypt, which represents a state of ignorance – mental and spiritual darkness. When we are in Egypt we are "without spiritual illumination" or higher understanding, often bound to conditions of fear, pain, lack, and dis-ease (SIOS, P.78). Into this condition of darkened thought comes Moses, "with promises of a better land" (metaphysical healing) and the resultant upliftment of our circumstances into greater freedom and abundance. In this second stage, Goldsmith explains, we experience expanded good on the human level but as with the Israelites wandering about in the wilderness there is still the " fluctuation between good and evil, plenty and lack, freedom and serfdom." We have not yet made "the transition to spiritual understanding" (P.79). Finally, like the Israelites led into the Promised Land by Joshua (a prototype of the Christ) we experience the third stage of growth: spiritual illumination. "Christ dawns in consciousness" (P.79) and we begin to live on a whole new stratum of our being. We have evolved from being under Law (Moses), to being wholly under Grace, which is the inner Christ, awakened and active in consciousness.

Moving into the New Testament in which Jesus Christ is the central figure, let us see if the universal concept of trinity is in evidence here, as well, in the events of his earthly life. For followers of mainstream Christian doctrine, Jesus' crucifixion and extreme agony on the Cross during which he took upon himself the sins of the world that humanity might be saved from sin, is the salient point, the culminating event of his thirty-three years and the fulfillment of his mission on earth. While the resurrection of the Lord is celebrated on Easter Sunday, and his ascension forty days later is acknowledged, it is for the most part Jesus' blood sacrifice on the cross of Calvary that most Christians focus upon as a dreadful but singular occurrence that took place over two thousand years ago.

Now students of New Thought learn that all of the characters and places in the Bible are outer depictions of conditions and states of consciousness within *us*. As we examine the significant events of Jesus' life, we understand that they are more than literal accounts of historical occurrences; they are, in fact, are *living symbolism,* representations of universal human experience. That is to say, we recognize them as metaphors for the phases of our own soul's journey. We discern that Jesus Christ can be viewed as "the archetypal human," embodying not only pain and suffering, but "the possibility of transcendence" (ANE, p.144). So as we look more deeply at the events surrounding the Crucifixion, we recognize something wonderful taking place – the presence of a Divine activity that far transcends the cruelty, betrayal and suffering of the Cross. We perceive the unfoldment of a grand design and discern its great *personal* significance.

Rather than focusing upon the Master's agony on the Cross, we remind ourselves that the Crucifixion was followed by Jesus' triumphant resurrection, and beyond that, his ascension into even higher planes. So instead of fixating upon Jesus' death as a unique event isolated in time, we realize that his crucifixion, resurrection and ascension correspond to three phases of consciousness that each one of us enacts and reenacts over and over in the course of our own evolution as spiritual beings. We recognize the presence and power of *trinity* at work!

We are *crucified* when we are in the depths of despair, sickness, and apparent betrayal. All is not lost, however, because crucifixion is not final. The Christ Principle within each of us is the power that when called upon, *resurrects* us from lower states of consciousness, and raises us above the trials of our thought-world so that each one of us can claim with Jesus: "Lo, I have overcome the world" (JN.16:33). Having moved through the tribulations of conditioned consciousness, we *ascend* into ever higher levels of awareness and degrees of self-realization. This is why Jesus, speaking as the Universal Christ, was able to make the promise: "If I (the resurrecting power of the Christ faculty in man) be lifted up... I will draw all men unto me" (JN.12:32).

So the Christ-story is our own story, a superb symbolic representation of the trinity of Being and a marvelous expression of the Holy Trinity of our own soul evolution.

CHAPTER 3

Where is Heaven?

Whosoever shall not receive the Kingdom of God
as a little child, shall in no wise enter in.
— Jesus Christ (Mark 10:15)

How hardly it is for a rich man to enter
the kingdom of Heaven (Matt.19:23).

Behold, the kingdom of God is within you (Luke 17:21).

Where indeed?!

In traditional Christianity, Heaven and its opposite realm, Hell, are viewed as literal localities, the ultimate destinations for individuals after physical death depending on the state of their souls at the time of earthly departure. Heaven is traditionally depicted as the celestial region where streets are paved with gold and angels float on clouds strumming harps, and like God Himself, is usually thought of as being "up there" somewhere in the Great Beyond. Conversely, Hell, the place of infernal torment to which an 'unsaved' individual is destined to spend eternity with no possibility of reprieve or escape, is usually thought of as "down there."

Now in New Thought we know that Heaven and Hell are not physical places (although all mental conditions do out-picture *as* external localities because thought is continuously externalizing itself), but essentially states of consciousness depicted *symbolically* as literal realms. Among its definitions of Hell, the *Metaphysical Bible Dictionary* describes it as a state of consciousness in which "man's mental processes are out of harmony with the Laws of Being" (p.271). Heaven, on the other hand is, metaphysically speaking, "a state of consciousness in which the soul and the body are in harmony with Divine Mind" (p. 266).

In *Find and Use Your Inner Power* Emmet Fox explains in simple terms our New Thought understanding of the two realms:

> When you have true peace of mind and an adequate understanding of life, you are already in heaven and when you are full of fear, anxiety, hatred, or physical pain, you are in hell (p. 48).

He goes on to remind us of the power we have consciously to select from moment to moment the thought-realm in which we would dwell:

> Whether you ...live in heaven or hell depends solely upon the kind of thinking you indulge in all day long. And fortunately, you can, by taking a little trouble, train yourself to make heaven-like thinking a constant habit (p.48).

In a colorful analogy, Fox writes that Heaven and Hell, like the saloons of the Old West, have "swing doors." By this, he means that we are not "locked in" to any negative circumstance; we can leave 'Hell' at any time, at the very instant we make the conscious decision to turn to God, Love, and Light. So the notion of being banished to a region called Hell for all eternity is an absurdity.

Nor do we in New Thought subscribe to the notion of "Judgment Day" – the dire final accounting for our sins awaiting us upon our demise that holds such terror for mainstream Christians. We claim that we are not punished *for* our sins but rather, *by* them. We reward or 'punish' (if that word can even be applied) ourselves "as we conform to or oppose the Laws of Life" (SR, P.11). The higher awareness of our indwelling spiritual nature, which is always operative, determines where balance needs to be restored and to the degree that we are open and receptive, lovingly guides us in re-establishing perfect alignment with Universal Law.

If we are going to tout the inerrancy of the Bible, as evangelical Christianity does, then we must look very closely at what the Scriptures have to say in the matter of Heaven and Hell. The word, Hell, is derived from the Hebrew 'sheol', meaning "the place of shadows." King David, author of the magnificent Book of Psalms asks:

> Whither shall I go from thy spirit and whither shall I flee from Thy Presence? If I ascend up into heaven, Thou art there; if I make my bed in Hell (Sheol), Behold, Thou art there (Psa. 139:1).

Here David affirms that even in the depths of what appears to be Hell – the shadow experiences of disease, pain and loss, we can never be separated from the loving Presence of our Father-Mother God. In this statement he clearly acknowledges the Omnipresence of God as "the loving watcher of our souls."

We know as metaphysicians that shadows and everything negative associated with them – disease, lack, inharmony – are merely manifestations of fear that flourish in the darkness of unillumined thought. They are *without substance*, because in Reality they have no divine dimension to support them. Fear is not an entity in itself, then, but rather, the absence of something positive – love, life, light, peace, and so forth. As figments of fearful imaginings, shadows must flee in the presence of light. When we turn on the light of Truth thinking, which means aligning ourselves in consciousness with the Divine Mind and the Light and Love that are eternal aspects of It – we recognize shadows for the phantoms they are and that recognition is often sufficient to dissolve any power the specters of Hell may hold for us. There can be no fear in Love because Love is the actual nature of Being itself.

The Bible has much to say about the power of love to dismantle and dissolve fear: "Fear not little flock, for it is your Father's good pleasure to give you the kingdom," Jesus tells his flock (LUKE12:32). And later in the New Testament we read these empowering affirmations of Absolute Truth:

> God has not given us the spirit of fear but of power and of love and of a sound mind (2 TIM 1:7).

> There is no fear in love; but perfect love casteth out fear: because fear hath torment. He that feareth is not made perfect in love (2 JN. 4:18).

In New Thought we know that heaven is not the static realm depicted by mainstream Christianity. As a state of consciousness, heaven has no parameters but is ever expanding into Infinity.

Jesus illustrates this point magnificently in a series of discourses on the nature of the kingdom in the form of parables. Although an in-depth interpretation of each parable is beyond the scope of this book, we will list a few of the best known in order to discern the unifying spiritual principle the Master is illustrating here: There are the parables of the mustard seed, the little bit of leaven required to raise the whole loaf, the treasure hidden in the field, the merchant seeking the jewel of the soul, and the net cast into the sea (MBD, P.266). In each of these stories, Jesus reveals that the kingdom of heaven – the consciousness of spiritual Truth in which peace and harmony prevail – always embodies the idea of *increase* and *expansion*.

Now let us examine what the Bible has to say about cultivating the demeanor and practices that are conducive to attaining a 'heavenly' or *expanded*, level of spiritual awareness. In the four gospels and the Sermon on the Mount, in particular, Jesus gives clear guidelines for "entering the kingdom." We will cite a few examples of his directives and then elucidate them briefly from a metaphysical standpoint:

Repent, for the kingdom of heaven is at hand (MATT.4:17).

In this statement, Jesus makes two things clear: first, that heaven not a far-distant realm but rather, exists right where we are. As Ernest Holmes writes in these comforting words:

The greatest good that can come to anyone is the forming within him of an absolute certainty of himself, and his relationship to the Universe, forever removing the sense of heaven as being outside of himself (SOM, P. 180).

Secondly, Jesus tells us that if we would come into the kingdom, i.e. awaken to the heavenly state of consciousness – we must repent. The word "repent" comes from the Latin *pentare,* meaning "to think." Quite simply, if we want to experience heaven, we must *re-think*, in other words, change our thinking to bring it into alignment with Divine Mind.

> Blessed are the poor in spirit, for theirs is the
> kingdom of heaven (Matt.5:3).

This proclamation from The Beatitudes, together with Jesus' assertion that it is hard for a rich man to enter the kingdom of heaven (Matt.19:23) has been interpreted by mainstream Christian denominations to mean that enjoying material wealth on earth is incompatible with entering the pearly gates after death. Poverty, on the other hand, traditionally has been celebrated as a virtue. If we are, in fact, meant to have abundance in every area of our lives, and we know in New Thought that we *are*, what then *does* Jesus' statement mean? In a brilliant interpretation from *Discover the Power within You*, Eric Butterworth provides the real meaning of this Beatitude: "To be poor in spirit means to empty yourself of the desire to exercise personal will in the quest for self-realization" (p.59). When personal will is relinquished, we become human transparencies through which the Divine Will can work and the kingdom of heaven — consciousness of All-Good – is truly ours.

> Not everyone shall enter into the kingdom of heaven...
> but he that doeth the will of my father which is in heaven.
> (Matt. 7:21)

Here again, Jesus emphasizes the importance of surrendering personal will and yielding to the greater Will of Divine Mind as a criterion for entering into the kingdom. Charles Fillmore writes that the will is the first of man's spiritual faculties to be developed, "the executive power of the human mind" that "moves to action all of the other faculties of the mind." (TPM, P.105, P.97). So relinquishing human will power is a significant achievement, spiritually speaking. But the rewards of yielding personal will (which often manifests as will-FULL-ness) to the greater Will of Divine Mind are more than commensurate with the self-discipline involved. The decision to "let go and let God" take the reins of our life ushers us directly into the kingdom (consciousness) of Perfect Good.

> Be ye perfect...even as your father in heaven is perfect.
> (MATT. 5:48)

To be perfect means to be whole and complete. Metaphysically speaking, it means to know ourselves as offspring of our heavenly Father, expressing in miniature all of the attributes of Being — the microcosm within the macrocosm. We are already whole and complete but we must know it consciously, and in this commandment, Jesus is indicating that our being perfect is an *attainable* reality.

> But lay up for yourselves treasures in heaven, where neither
> moth nor rust doth corrupt (MATT.6:20).

Since we recognize that metaphysically, heaven always refers to the mind or mental realm, we understand that Jesus is reminding us here that the only things to be sought after, the only things which are enduring are the treasures – our thoughts of Truth – which we accumulate in consciousness. It is our consciousness of Truth that is the pearl of great price, our eternal treasure in heaven.

> For if ye forgive men their trespasses, your heavenly father
> will also forgive you (Matt. 6:14).

Jesus tells us here, by implication, that withholding forgiveness holds us in bondage to lesser states of being, while forgiveness of self and others unties God's hands, releasing us from the prison of our own making and allowing Universal Law to operate on our behalf. Forgiveness is absolutely essential to entering that state of harmony, peace, and all-around well-being Jesus calls the kingdom of heaven. Gerald Jampolsky, medical doctor, author and student of *A Course in Miracles,* writes in a book on the subject entitled simply *Forgiveness* that "Forgiveness is the greatest healer of all." Forgiveness is the vehicle through which we transcend states of discord and rise into that experience of "the peace that passes understanding" we know as heaven.

> Except ye become as little children, ye shall not enter into
> the kingdom of heaven (Matt. 18:3).

In this familiar, oft-quoted Bible verse, Jesus tells us that in order to enter the Kingdom, we must be as open, receptive, and trusting as a little child. It is the trust born of love, the quality of *implicit* trust a child has in its earthly father that opens the floodgates of heaven and baptizes us with heavenly peace. Brother Mandus, late founder of the World Healing Crusade in England, speaks of the beautiful experience of entering the peace of God as a little child in the following excerpt from a healing meditation:

> There IS a stillness that is beyond all human understanding, the deep deep stillness in which the peace of God flows so tenderly, so joyously into our midst... It begins best when we are so simple, like little children, when we accept the Almighty Presence as the great Reality, when we go beyond the ifs and the buts and the questioning, when we take Christ at His word, when we know that we live and move and have our being IN the Almightiness of God, that the very life within us is the Life of God Himself. Then we can become humble and simple with a childlike trust.
>
> And immediately when we pray like that, the Father brings us unto His harmony. And when you consider that all the tensions of life, the problems, the pains, the disease of mind or body are states of discord, you can begin to see that when we abide in the secret place of the Most High, in the stillness of the Holy Spirit, peace is the opposite of the tension or the discord. Peace of Mind is more necessary to us today than anything else. And that peace is the peace which Jesus spoke about, the peace that is beyond human understanding. It is the Peace of the Holy Spirit in which allthings flow back to their central harmony. Be still.
>
> Peace of God. You can feel it, such a loving and gentle calmness; it flows through the whole of your being. Feel it so effortlessly. All the tensions flow right out of your body. You are enfolded in the great peace of God. It's such a lovely feeling, the feeling of the deep deep stillness.

It comes from the very deeps of your being and all around you is the Glory of God (c.1975).

This is the kingdom – the heavenly consciousness – awaiting us when we become as little children – innocent, pure in heart and centered in the ever-expanding awareness that we are surrounded, enfolded and upheld by Infinite Love, Infinite Life, and Infinite Power.

And so it is that as we embrace the Truth of Being and endeavor to live by the Laws of Being, our evolution as spiritual beings knows no bounds. We continue to grow and evolve in an unending and glorious experience of soul unfoldment. This is what it means to dwell in the kingdom of heaven.

CHAPTER 4

The Only Begotten Son

Jesus Christ, the same, yesterday, today, and forever (Heb. 13:8).

...Christ in you, the hope of glory (Col. 1:27).

To realize within oneself a Divine Presence, a perfect
Person, Is to recognize the Christ.
— Ernest Holmes, *The Science of Mind*

For God so loved the world, he gave His only begotten Son
that whosoever should believe on him should not perish
but have everlasting life (John 3:16).

What persons raised in a Christian household did not grow
up hearing the oft-quoted Scripture directly above as the basis
for their salvation through the blood sacrifice and vicarious
atonement of Jesus Christ on the Cross?

Within the tenets of mainstream Christianity, Jesus Christ
holds the distinction of being the only divine Son of God,
immaculately conceived, entirely without sin, singularly

endowed with miraculous powers and bearing the unique title "Savior of Mankind." The rest of humanity, on the other hand, is held to be under the stain of Original Sin, Adam and Eve's initial defiance of God in the Garden of Eden, and is therefore inherently unregenerate, or "born in sin," as fundamentalists claim. Jesus' proclamation "I AM the way, the truth, and the life...no man cometh unto the father but by me" (JN.14:6) has been used throughout Christendom to substantiate the unique divinity of Jesus and his role as Savior of mankind and reinforce the intrinsically fallen nature of humanity at large.

The metaphysical teachings of New Thought present a far more uplifting conception of humankind, however, one that bridges the apparent gap between the supreme divinity of Jesus and the worm-of-the-dust status of everyone else. In *Spirits in Rebellion,* Charles S. Braden's comprehensive volume tracing the origin, growth and philosophy of the New Thought movement, he writes that New Thought believes in a divine humanity, a "human brotherhood with a divine Fatherhood" and claims that "the children of men are living souls *now*, Children of God... spiritual citizens of a divine universe" (SR,P.10). New Thought – metaphysical Christianity – proclaims the inherent *goodness* of man. In fact, New Thought teachings celebrate man's intrinsic divinity, the Divine spark within him, that while perhaps not in full expression, nevertheless constitutes his true nature.

Unlike the main Christian denominations, metaphysical Christianity does not teach that man is born in sin. Rather, we say with Kenneth Carey in the wonderful little volume entitled *The Starseed Transmissions,* that "we are born daily into the Presence of God" (ST,P.15). New Thought recognizes man's true nature as divine and celebrates his untapped divine potential. Carey tells us that "as the Christ, the only begotten consciousness of the Father, [we] have been given a number of remarkable qualities" (p.18). We are "gods in embryo," metaphysicians declare, differing from Jesus not in our essential nature, but only in the *degree* to which we are expressing our inherent spiritual faculties. In the course of living we are ever in the process of awakening to our illustrious divine heritage and allowing it to unfold from within until it is revealed in full splendor upon the manifest plane.

It is here that we must make a vital distinction, one which is overlooked, misunderstood or even denied by practitioners of mainstream Christianity but is clearly recognized by adherents of the New Thought philosophy. Jesus and Christ are not synonymous. It is a differentiation that is vital to understanding who Jesus was and essential to comprehending the significance of his teachings, his ministry and his legacy. Jesus was the name given to the man of Galilee, his historical human identity. "Christ" however, is not a proper name; it is a *designation* meaning "the anointed one." It represents recognition of the supreme spiritual stature of the historical man, Jesus.

As metaphysicians we have always grasped the distinction between *Jesus*, the man of Nazareth, and *the Christ principle* which Jesus embodied and brought into full flowering as the *actualization* of that potential which is within each of us. Jesus himself acknowledged the difference between the two terms, referring to *himself* as both Son of God (the divine aspect of his nature) *and* Son of Man (the human aspect). The terms represent two phases of his being and indeed of our *own* being.

The entire focus of Jesus' ministry – both through his teachings and in the great works that he did – was to embody and illustrate the distinction between the two aspects of his nature, because it was absolutely essential to our own understanding of who *we* are – spiritual beings (the Christ of us) expressing through human forms. In *Power through Constructive Thinking* Emmet Fox calls our inherent spiritual potential, our own Christ faculty, "The Wonder Child", because like a child nurtured in its mother's womb, it is not yet fully mature, but in the process of development while lovingly enfolded in the matrix of the soul. There, under the aegis of God's love and protection, the Christ-child, our individual spiritual selfhood, gradually but steadily grows in strength and maturity until the day comes when it is ready to be fully revealed upon the plane of manifestation (PTCT, pp.3-4).

It should be recognized, however, that the evolved soul which was Jesus the man, lived in such perfect attunement with the Divine Source he called "the Father", that he was in fact a Christed being. Jesus lived in full conscious awareness of his Oneness with God so within him, the two aspects of his nature – the human and the divine – were fused, blended in perfect harmony and synchronization. He could truthfully say "I and my Father are One" because he had fully transcended any sense of self, separate and apart from his God-Self. He claimed that he was in the Father and the Father in him. Even as he made such declarations of Oneness, though, he acknowledged that "the Father is greater than ALL"(JN.10:29), meaning that he was aware of himself as individualized being *within* Universal Being, the part within the whole, embodying in particularized form all of the *qualities* of the Whole. This awareness is the goal we are seeking.

Now let's look more closely at what is meant by the title "Christ" in the New Thought philosophy. Various metaphysical groups interpret the term in slightly different ways but each group's explanation complements the others. In his *Dore Lectures*, Thomas Troward, the British Judge and lecturer on Mental Science in the early years of the 20th century, puts forth this understanding of the Son's (Christ's) relation to the Father: "Christ is the Archetypal Idea in the All-Creating Mind…and so we arrive at the Christ-Idea as a universal Principle" (DORE, P. 65). In *The Hidden Power* he amplifies this idea:

> The Christ conception, the realization of the Christ principle, as exhibited in the Christ person, brings you in touch with the personal element in the Universal Spirit, the divine creative, first-moving spirit of the Universe (P.44).

Prominent metaphysicians who succeeded Troward have experienced the same insight into the nature of the Christ Principle and its relation to the individual, Jesus of Nazareth, and described the relationship in slightly different, but complementary, ways. Charles Fillmore clarifies what Jesus was trying to convey to his followers in these words:

> I feel sure that Jesus Christ did not wish to be worshiped as a personal man in a historical setting. He yearned to have all men join with him in a glorious realization of the spiritual sonship of *all*. (Unity recording)

Like the New Thought teachers before him, Ernest Holmes of Religious Science (CSL) also grasped the distinction between the human being, Jesus, and the title "Christ." In *The Science of Mind* he defines Christ as "the Word of God in and through man" and states that "the Christ knows his individuality is indestructible, that he is an eternal Being, living forever in the bosom of the

Father" (SOM, P.379). Each one of us "puts on Christ" he writes, "to the degree that [we] surrender a limited sense of life to the Divine realization of wholeness and unity with Good, Spirit, God" (PP. 578-79).

In the book *Conscious Union with God*, Joel Goldsmith explains the term "Christ" this way:

> The Christ really and truly is one's individual identity, one's real being. The Christ is individual consciousness when it has been purged of all love, fear or hate of error of any nature. When you no longer love, fear or hate error in any form, you are Christ Consciousness... Just as we have to arrive at an understanding of God appearing as man, so we also have to realize Christ as immanent (indwelling), as the Christ of our own being, the Christ of our own consciousness (P.112).

As Eckhart Tolle says in his revolutionary best-seller *The Power of Now*, "Never personalize Christ. Don't make Christ into a form identity." Christ refers to our indwelling divinity, "regardless of whether [we] are conscious of it or not" (P.104). Jesus, on the other hand, was the fully realized expression of Christ Consciousness in individualized form. This same consciousness is the Divine Presence or essence of each of us, the Truth of our being, that Principle which "is the same, yesterday, today, and forever" (HEB.13:8).

We find biblical support for our metaphysical understanding of the Christ Ideal – the notion of Universal Sonship – as the eternal foundation of man's intrinsic worth. The most succinct, yet profound revelation of man's indwelling divinity is found in Jesus' own question to his disciples: "Does not your scripture say, ye are gods and sons of the most high?" (PSA.82:6 AND JN.10:34)

Later in the New Testament, the Apostle Paul writes that man's innate worth, goodness, and divinity, which he calls the 'mystery' of man's true identity, "the great secret hidden through the ages", is "Christ in you, the hope of glory" (Col. 1:27). Note that Paul does not say "Jesus in you, the hope of glory" but rather Christ, the eternal Principle of wholeness and *holy*-ness, dwelling within each one of us as our own divine heritage and potential. In another passage, Paul tells us that if we are children of God, then we are heirs, "heirs of God and *joint-heirs* with Christ" (Rom.8:17). When Paul states that "If any man be in Christ, he is a new creature," (2Cor.5:17) he is declaring that when we are established at the *Christ level* of awareness we are wholly transformed.

As referenced earlier, the single most quoted assertion of the Master: "I AM the way, the truth and the life…no man cometh unto the father but by me" has been used by fundamentalist Christians to validate their claim that in order to be *saved*, we must believe in the personhood of Jesus as the only ticket to salvation and eternity in heaven. This declaration has been used to disparage other religions as false doctrines while proclaiming the unique divinity of Jesus and the superiority of Christianity. We must understand, however, that Jesus is speaking here from the level of fully awakened spiritual awareness, what we metaphysicians often call Christ Consciousness – the divine dimension of his being and indeed, of our *own* being. Charles Fillmore expresses the idea of man's innate divinity so well in this statement from an early Unity recording:

> I do not believe that Jesus Christ meant that *he* was the way, but he pointed to the Christ, the perfect spiritual man within him, as the way.

So when we hear fundamentalist Christians speak of "The Second Coming" of Christ, we in New Thought know that we are not expecting the man Jesus to appear momentarily in the clouds, wearing robe and sandals, to take up his elect while the remainder of humanity is left to flounder and die. With our understanding of the deeper implications of the second coming of Christ, we recognize that the term refers to the awakening of Christ consciousness on a universal scale. For Eckhart Tolle, the "second coming" represents the shift from time (ego) to Presence (Being) that is already taking place at the collective level. As the author says, Jesus was "a vehicle for the pure consciousness" (PON, P.104) that is Christ and this same consciousness is the Divine Presence or essence of each of us, the Truth of our being, that Principle which "is the same, yesterday, today, and forever."

In her wonderful DVD series entitled *The Book of Co-Creation,* Barbara Marx Hubbard claims that Jesus now exists "in total Christ Consciousness, which is a frequency band of awareness that is open to all who imagine themselves as [Christ], whatever name they may use." As we grow in spiritual understanding, we begin to move away from the idea of the individual named Jesus as our personal Savior and come to *realize* – make real to our understanding – that it is the Christ Principle wholly mature and expressing in completeness through Jesus, a spiritual faculty shared by each one of us as potential Christs, that constitutes our salvation.

New Thought folks get the distinction!

CHAPTER 5

Born-Again – or Born *Anew*?

Except a man be born again he cannot see the
Kingdom of God (Jn. 3:3).

Except a man be born of water and of the spirit,
he cannot enter into the Kingdom of God (Jn.3:5).

The new birth is [man's] realization of his spiritual identity
with the fullness of power and glory that follows.
— Charles Fillmore, *The Revealing Word*

In the teachings of fundamentalist Christianity, being "born again" is considered to be *the* criterion by which a soul is deemed either worthy or unfit to enter the kingdom of Heaven after physical death. From Sunday morning pulpits all over Christendom preachers of mainstream denominations invite parishioners to confess Jesus Christ as their personal Savior (is there any other kind?!). Televangelists of all stripes offer the opportunity for viewers to secure sure access to the pearly gates by declaring that they must repent of their sins and "accept the

Lord." It is thought that by simply mouthing these words one is delivered automatically from the torment of an eternity in Hell and guaranteed a place near the heavenly throne.

It is unfortunate that the term "born again" has been so misunderstood and mis-used. Experiencing a spiritual conversion is not something one shouts from the rooftops and uses to convince others that he is "saved" and therefore, guaranteed a spot in Heaven after death. The true meaning of being born again is so much more profound than the mere act of confessing verbally one's belief in the sovereignty of Jesus as the Lord of one's life. Adherents of New Thought understand that spiritual rebirth is a very interior experience, a revelation of Truth that takes place in the inner sanctum of one's being. The new birth is the *re-awakening* to the Truth of one's divinity – the conscious revelation of one's unity with the Source.

The *Metaphysical Bible Dictionary* defines the awakening experience this way:

> [The new birth] is the change from carnal to spiritual consciousness through the begetting and quickening power of the word of Truth …in man's inner consciousness the process of being born anew includes the whole of man – spirit, soul, and body (p.481).

Thus we see that true spiritual conversion is an interior *transformational* experience that cannot be induced by mere verbal mumbo-jumbo. Metaphysicians understand that being born again really means being born *anew,* that it means dying utterly to the self one has been and allowing the greater self, the tremendous spiritual potential of one's being, which we often refer to as the Christ-Self, to be brought forth – *birthed*, if you will, upon the manifest plane. Emmet Fox puts it this way:

> [To be born again] is to come into truth with your whole body, to bring every conscious thought and belief to the touchstone of Divine Intelligence and Divine Love. It is to reject every single thing, mental or physical, that does not square with that standard. It is to revise every opinion, every habit of thought, every policy, every branch of practical conduct, without any exception whatever. This of course is something absolutely tremendous. It is no mere spring cleaning of the soul. It is nothing less than a wholesale tearing down and rebuilding of the entire house (PTCT,p.148).

In New Thought, we know that the term *house* stands for consciousness, so the tearing down and rebuilding of one's house means the entire dismantling and restructuring of one's consciousness that it may truly be filled with Light. In his essay on *Light and Salvation* Dr. Fox goes on to say of being born-again:

> The new birth…means that you clearly understand and definitely accept the fact that nothing matters except attunement with God. When you can honestly say "I realize now that nothing really matters except that I get my conscious attunement with God – because when I have that, everything else will follow, and until I do get that, nothing else can be right, and I am going to make everything else secondary to that," then you have really experienced the new birth (i.e. been "saved") whether the realization itself has arrived yet or not (PTCT, pp.82-83.).

The Bible teaches the new birth experience throughout its pages by emphasizing the newness of being that arises from a change of thought. "As [a man] thinketh in his heart (i.e. with feeling and conviction), so is he", King Solomon in his wisdom and recognition of spiritual verities, writes in the Old Testament Book of Proverbs (23:7).

In the New Testament, Jesus describes the requirement for the new birth experience in the quotation that began this chapter: "Except a man be born of water and [of] the Spirit, he cannot enter the Kingdom of God" (Jn. 3:5). Like bathing in the physical ocean, spiritual rebirth is an experience of *total* immersion in the Divine − the sea of pure Spirit − that must take place if one is to enter the Kingdom (consciousness) of God. In this state of conscious oneness with the Divine Source, there is no longer a separate individual consciousness; the division between God and man has blurred and there is only Oneness. Ernest Holmes points out, however, that we cannot be born of the Spirit unless we do the *will* of the Spirit, which is "goodness, peace, mercy, justice, and truth" (SOM, p.379).

Being born again means, as the Apostle Paul declares in the early decades after Jesus' transition (and as Emmet Fox would reiterate centuries later), "dying daily" (1Cor. 5:31) to every flaw of character, every prejudice, every petty form of deceit and selfishness; it signifies the willingness to give up anything and everything that would stand in the way of total spiritual transformation. Dr. Fox goes on to say that because of the high price extracted by the process of totally surrendering one's sense of a separate human identity, "all but the very strongest spirits shirk it." He reminds us, however, that we do not get very far, spiritually speaking, without being prepared to "slay the present man" that the new spiritual being may be born (p.148).

Paul writes in his epistle to the Corinthians: "Therefore if any man [be] in Christ, [he is] a new creature: old things are passed away; behold, all things are become new" (2Cor.5:17). When the inner Christ takes dominion, we are renewed *from within* in spirit, mind, emotions, and body. Everything that characterized the former state of consciousness is no more. Again, in the Revelation of the Christ to John the Divine we read "Behold, I maketh all things *new*" (Rev. 21:5). We metaphysicians understand the deeper implications of this statement to mean that in the transforming activity of rebirth, old things (states of consciousness) are as waters that have passed away. We start with a clean slate from this point.

In *The Varieties of Religious Experience*, William James recounts the experience of a young man in 1739, long beset by periods of intense "mournful melancholy", awakening to the new awareness of splendor and joy that we call being born anew:

> I thought that the Spirit of God had quite left me. [I was] disconsolate, as if there was nothing in heaven or earth that could make me happy. Having been thus endeavoring to pray...for nearly half an hour; then as I was walking in a thick grove, unspeakable glory seemed to open to the apprehension of my soul. I do not mean any external brightness, nor any imagination of a body of light, but it was a new inward apprehension or view, such as I never had before...It appeared to be divine glory. My soul rejoiced with joy unspeakable to see such a God , such a glorious Divine Being...I continued in this state of inward joy, peace and astonishing till near dark without any sensible abatement...I felt myself in a new world, and every thing about me appeared with a different aspect from what it was wont to do (p.181).

In the new higher state of consciousness described by the preceding excerpt – which is but one instance of a timeless universal human experience – we look upon the world with new eyes, so that everything truly does take on a fresh aspect.

Thus, we see that with the inner Christ on the throne, our metamorphosis – *rebirth* – is total, complete, and eternal. Like the earthbound caterpillar's emergence from the chrysalis of limitation to the shimmering upward dance of the butterfly, we too are born again – born *anew* – into a whole new level of radiant Life.

CHAPTER 6

What is Salvation?

In returning and rest shall ye be saved (Isa.30:15).

There is no salvation outside of conscious cooperation
with the Infinite.
— Ernest Holmes, *The Science of Mind*

Salvation is not just a theological concept. It is
metaphysical and psychological as well. The only thing
to be saved from is our own fear-based thinking.
— Marianne Williamson, on her Facebook page

Followers of traditional Christianity place the need for
salvation at the very epicenter of their spiritual concerns. The
deep desire for salvation and the fear of *not* being saved are at the
crux of every believer's seeking. Before looking more deeply
into the meaning of salvation as we in New Thought understand
the term, let us look at the origin of the word and its various
meanings.

SALVATION, as defined by Merriam Webster: from the Latin root *salvare*, meaning *to save*.

1. a: deliverance from the power and effects of sin
    b: the agent or means that effects salvation
    c: Christian Science : [Salvation is] the realization of the supremacy of infinite Mind over all, bringing with it the destruction of the illusion of sin, sickness, and death

2. liberation from ignorance or illusion

3. a: preservation from destruction or failure
    b: deliverance from danger or difficulty

The first definition that appears above tallies exactly with the meaning of salvation as taught in traditional Christian dogma: "deliverance from the power and effects of sin." This is the view held by most people who call themselves Christians and it is the reason that salvation, as defined by traditional Christians, is a matter of life and death in the most literal sense of the word. But what exactly is it that they are saved *from*? To answer this question we must look back briefly at the history of man's entry onto the scene as described in the Book of Genesis, and interpreted by fundamentalist Christianity as a literal historical event that took place six thousand years ago.

In the familiar creation story, the first man and woman, Adam and Eve, disobeyed God when they ate of the forbidden fruit from the tree of the knowledge of good and evil in the Garden of Eden. In this act of defiance, they fell from grace, ushered in a world of sin and tribulation and consigned themselves and everyone who came after them to the certainty of eternal damnation after death. This initial disobedience, called by traditional Christians "Original Sin", as cited in a preceding chapter, is the stain with which they believe all the descendants of the first man and woman are tainted.

In Christian doctrine, the only possibility of redemption for human beings was for God to send a Savior who, if they believed in him, would rescue their souls from the dire fate of eternal torment in Hell and assure them safe passage into Heaven. This is the meaning of salvation as understood by most adherents of Christian dogma. While asserting that they are *saved* here and now, however, the actual experience of salvation is, for Christian fundamentalists, a blissful spiritual condition that is promised for some future time after physical death, depending upon their individual acceptance of Jesus Christ, as noted earlier, as their personal Savior. From this, we can see why salvation holds such a central position in their theology.

But in reading the dictionary definitions above, we discover the far more inclusive definition of *salvation* found in Christian Science, one that dovetails neatly with the way sin and salvation are viewed in the New Thought philosophy:

> [Salvation is] the realization of the supremacy of infinite Mind over all, bringing with it the destruction of the illusion of sin, sickness, and death.

Here we see that God as Infinite Mind is All-in-All; everything that appears to contradict this Truth is simply an illusion that needs to be dissolved at the level of thought.

In *The Revealing Word*, Charles Fillmore defines sin as "man's failure to express the attributes of Being – life, love, intelligence, wisdom and the other God-qualities." As is often said in metaphysical circles, sin is "missing the mark", in other words, "falling short of divine perfection". Interestingly, in both Latin and Spanish the word 'sin' means *without,* so to be *in sin* means simply that for the moment we believe ourselves to be outside of – without — our Divine Source and are functioning from that consciousness of separation.

If sin is merely a matter of believing ourselves to be apart from God, how then are we *saved*? Fillmore goes on to say that since sin, or *error,* is in the mind, it must be "redeemed by a mental process, by going into the silence [of prayer]. Error is brought into the light of Spirit and then transformed into a constructive force." Salvation, then, "comes *solely* as the result of redemption… an inner overcoming, a change in consciousness, a cleansing of the mind through Christ, from thoughts of evil (duality)" (TRW, P.179).

We find support for Fillmore's understanding of salvation as "the restitution of man to his spiritual birthright" (P. 137) in the words of the New Testament. Paul declares in the book of Romans "Be ye *transformed* by the renewal of your mind" (ROM. 12:2). When the necessary correction is made at the thought-level, all external conditions and circumstances begin to adjust themselves accordingly, sometimes in miraculous ways. This is real transformation and it is indeed a 'saving' experience.

Thus, we see that in New Thought salvation encompasses much more than rescuing the human spirit from perpetual damnation after physical death. Just as real prosperity includes much more than money, so does true salvation embody more than retrieving the soul from eternity in Hell. Salvation means "all-around harmony and demonstration," Emmet Fox claims in his illuminating essay on *Light and Salvation* (PTCT, P.79), freedom from the darkness of mental ignorance and bondage to the appearance of sickness, poverty, and any other form of limitation. Salvation – our liberation from ignorance or illusion as stated above in dictionary definition #2 – embraces mental and physical well-being, peace, abundance, fulfillment in every area of life, as Dr. Fox claims.

Eckhart Tolle enlarges upon Fox's understanding that salvation encompasses much more than the limited meaning it holds in mainstream Christianity. In *The Power of Now* he writes that salvation means knowing God as the Truth of our own being, our own essential nature as an inseparable part of the "timeless, formless One life":

> True salvation is fulfillment, peace, life in all its fullness. It is to be who you are, to feel within you the good that has no opposite, the joy of Being that depends on nothing outside itself. It is not felt as a passing experience but as an abiding presence. In theistic language, it is to "know God" – not as something outside you but as your own innermost essence. It is to know yourself as an inseparable part of the timeless and formless One life from which all that exists has its being (PON, p. 146).

"True salvation", the author continues, "is a state of freedom – from fear, from suffering, from a perceived state of lack and insufficiency...It is freedom from compulsive thinking, from negativity and above all from past and future as a psychological need" (p. 146). Salvation takes place *continuously* as we raise our thought-stream above the level of consciousness where negative circumstances appear to hold sway.

And most significantly, salvation – the fullness of life that is ours as we feel the joy of Being as an abiding Presence – is available to us in the present moment. In *Mightier than Circumstance* Unity author Frank B. Whitney writes:

> God promises you that if you turn to him, he will bring his justice right to you without delay, He promises you that if you will believe on Him he will adjust the differences between you and your neighbor immediately. He promises that the right thing will be done in your life without delay. He promises that He will correct any situation that needs correcting. He promises to take over all your troubles and guarantees to put all your affairs in perfect order. When? Without tarrying. Right now and here (P.55).

Nowhere is it stated, or even implied, in the Bible that salvation can only be achieved at a future date! The teachings of both the Old and New Testaments bear out the notion that salvation is not for a future time after death, but rather a spiritual state that is *continuously and instantaneously* available to us now. Throughout its pages, the Bible speaks of the immediacy of God's help, His deliverance in every need and in all situations. "God *is* a very present help in trouble," Psalm 46:1 proclaims and in Isaiah we find this assurance: "I bring thee near my righteousness; it shall not be far off and my salvation shall not tarry (Is. 46:13)." In Psalm 27 we read:

> The Lord is my light and my salvation; whom shall I fear?
> The Lord is the strength of my life; of whom
> shall I be afraid (PSA.27:1).

In the quotation directly above, we note that the word "light" precedes the word "salvation." This is significant because it tells us that as we recognize God, the Lord (Law) of our being, our own *IAM*, as sovereign in our life, our consciousness becomes filled with Light. In other words, it is the realization of Truth – our own "light bulb moment" when the awareness of our true nature as spiritual beings dawns within consciousness – that saves us. In this illumined awareness, we recognize our innate freedom and are thus liberated from bondage to all false states of consciousness which we call "Hell." We assert the dominion and mastery that are within us and begin to experience the exalted level of consciousness that can rightfully be called Heaven.

In Paul's letter to the Corinthians he proclaims "Now is the accepted time. Now is the day of salvation" (2 Cor. 6:2). Jesus recognized that both the past and the future are, in truth, illusions; he knew that all we ever have is the present moment and that NOW, therefore, is the only time in which we can be *saved*. Thus, the entire thrust of his earthly ministry was present-moment centered. He adjured us to release the past in his counsel to one of the disciples, "Let the dead [past] bury its dead" (Matt.8:22). Likewise, he taught us (in the Sermon on the Mount) to release anxiety about the future when he advised "Take no thought for the morrow, for the morrow shall take thought for the things of itself" and in a statement uttered often by my earthly father, "Sufficient unto the day is the evil [problems and challenges] thereof" (Matt.6:34).

Ernest Holmes reminds us: "There is no salvation apart from our conscious cooperation with the Law." In an excerpt from one of the quotations that began this chapter: "In returning and rest shall ye be saved" (Isa.30:15), we see that in the simple act of turning in thought away from any negative claim and resting in the awareness of God's Presence in the situation – evidence of our willingness to cooperate with the Law of our being, we are immediately lifted up, *saved* – saved from whatever consequences we may have invited by taking the negative appearance at face value.

While in the midst of writing this chapter, I had one of those delightful synchronicities that sometimes occurs when we are in the midst of a spiritual endeavor and illuminates beautifully the point we are trying to make. I was taking a break from writing to check my Facebook page when the following quote from Eckhart Tolle jumped out at me:

> You are the light of the world. You are the consciousness that illuminates the world. Know yourself as that and that's freedom, liberation, awakening, the end of suffering and madness. And it's happening right now.

Have you ever heard of a more perfect way to define salvation? And as Tolle's words echo the words of the Scriptures, it is happening *right now.* Now is the only time salvation can occur because now is the only time there is. It cannot exist in any future time or dimension because there *is* only Now. Therefore, salvation must be *now* or it is not at all.

Salvation, then, is not something that awaits the chosen few at some undefined point in the Hereafter, but a spiritual awareness that embraces ALL, *now.*

CHAPTER 7

Holy Communion

I am the living bread (Jn.6:48).

He that eateth my flesh and drinketh my blood
dwelleth in me and I in him (Jn.6:56).

Deeper is the silence of the place of peace within you....
where you commune with God.

— James Dillet Freeman, *The Place of the Silence*

The sacrament of Holy Communion is considered to be
among the most solemn and sacred of all the rituals in the
traditional denominations of the Christian Church. In this
religious rite, based upon the actions of Jesus at the Last Supper
where he instructs his disciples to partake of his body and blood
in remembrance of him, participants gather at the altar during a
church service to reenact the events of that night. The officiating
clergyman distributes a wafer to each congregant, representing the
body of Jesus, and pours from a chalice of wine, representing the
blood of Jesus Christ "shed for the remission of sins" (Matt.26:28).

Many Christians believe that during the Eucharist ceremony, the bread or wafer and the wine are transformed miraculously into the actual body and blood of Jesus Christ by a mystical process called *transubstantiation.*

Moving beyond the literal acceptance of the events of the last night of Jesus' earthly sojourn let's examine them from a deeper metaphysical standpoint. In this book, we have already seen that New Thought practitioners recognize the distinction between the historical man Jesus and the Christ that indwelt him as the eternal pattern for the individual, the glorious universal template of perfection for all of humankind.

Continuing to elucidate Biblical symbolism, we know that throughout the Bible, the word "bread" is used to represent Spiritual substance, the eternal living essence that each of us draws upon in prayer for sustenance and strength. "Give us our daily bread", we say from the Lord's Prayer (MATT. 6:11). "Cast your bread upon the waters", Jesus instructs in one passage, and in another speaking as the Christ, declares "I AM that bread of life"(JN. 6:51). We understand that the liquid counterpart of the communion bread, the wine representing the blood of Jesus, stands for the life-force that courses through our being.

And, as we have discussed already, the term "Christ" as used throughout the New Testament, denotes the eternal spiritual principle within each one of us, which is in Truth our real identity. So as we in New Thought examine the account of the Last Supper found in the gospel of John, we intuitively grasp the metaphysical meaning of Jesus' actions at the table and are thus able to interpret the sacrament of Holy Communion on a far deeper level, a level which has profound personal significance for each one of us.

We understand that all the events in the life of the historical Jesus were representative of universal human experience, so when Jesus instructs his twelve disciples gathered at the Last Supper to reenact the communion ceremony after his departure, we discern that he is in fact acting from the vantage point of the Christ faculty within each person. When he speaks the words: "This is my body" and "this is my blood...this do in remembrance of me", we know he is speaking as the Christ Principle eternally operative when *activated* by man at the level of Mind.

> Within man is an altar where the Christ is holding religious
> services at all times.
>
> — CHARLES FILLMORE

The Christ, speaking through Jesus at The Last Supper, is stating an eternal truth: that the Universal Substance symbolized by the communion bread is what nourishes and sustains us, and the accelerated ethers of Christ-Consciousness into which we tap during higher states of awareness such as meditation, symbolized by the wine, comprise the very life-force that flows through our being. It is the *inner* sacrament of partaking of the eternal nourishment of the Spirit that we are to reenact. *This* is the true significance of the sacrament of Holy Communion and it is indeed a holy activity, because through it, we re-affirm the Whole-ness – Holy-ness – of our being and our own inherent capacity for transfiguration.

In *The Art of Meditation,* Joel Goldsmith offers this understanding of the true meaning of Holy Communion:

Our Father has imparted to us Himself. In the realization of our true identity, we partake of the body of God: that is eating the Body, and drinking the Blood. " 'I have meat to eat that ye know not of." *I* can give you life—waters that spring into life eternal –invisible waters, invisible wine, invisible meat." This is partaking of the living God, the living Word, and watching the Word become flesh, and dwell among us – God incarnate in the flesh (P.74).

Unity writer Frances Foulks expresses the metaphysical interpretation of Holy Communion in these words:

The more often we enter in (in consciousness) and in mind lay hold of the perfect pattern or God idea of man the less attention and consideration we shall need to give to the material body. In this *communion* we shall touch the mystical Christ-body and Christ will give us to eat of his substance and drink of his life. We shall build again a spiritual body immune from disease which will not suffer pain or become weak and helpless. To commune with this real body is to make the outer earth garment like it. It was after such communion that the Master was transfigured. It will be in some such way that we too shall become transfigured, transformed, renewed. Then we shall glorify God in our body (*Effectual Prayer,* p. 39).

It is important to bear in mind that true *communion* – the merging of human consciousness with the Godhead – is supremely personal in nature, an *interior* experience, one that takes place within the innermost sanctuary of one's soul. Since, as Charles Filmore knew "there is within man an altar where the Christ is holding religious services at all times," union with the Divine can take place anywhere and at any time one is in conscious attunement with one's indwelling Lord. It does not depend on anyone's being in a church setting or taking part in a ritual administered by a third party designated as a church official or authority, such as a clergyman. The only intermediary needed to experience Holy Communion is the indwelling Christ, the mystical Christ, and it is *Its* office to do the work of transubstantiation.

CHAPTER 8

What About Prayer?

God is Spirit ... and they that worship Him must worship
Him in Spirit and Truth (JN. 4:24).

Any mental activity which enables us to raise the spiritual
standard of the soul is a form of prayer.

— EMMET FOX, *Power through Constructive Thinking*

Stillness is the language God speaks and everything
else is a bad translation.

— ECKHART TOLLE, *A New Earth*

The impetus to pray — to connect intimately with something
greater than oneself — whatever one conceives that Something
to be — is a universal impulse within the human soul. Since the
inception of humankind on this planet, people have prayed in all
manner of ways, and under every conceivable circumstance. As
we saw in the first chapter on the nature of God, in the main
denominations of Christianity the Supreme Being is regarded as
remote, external and somewhat unresponsive to human needs.

Man must therefore implore, beg and placate God in various ways in order to have any expectation of answered prayer, and even then, there is no assurance of divinely bestowed fulfillment.

Approaches to the Supreme Being have traditionally taken one of several forms designed to soften the heart of an indifferent or wrathful Deity and secure Divine favor: formal prayers which are memorized and recited mechanically with little thought or feeling, attempts at appeasing God through elaborate rituals and acts of propitiation, bargaining with God in hopes of finding favor with the deity, or *supplicatory* prayers sent 'upward' to an external God in the hope that He will hear them and be moved to answer them — if He (and the anthropomorphic God has always been thought of as male) determines that they are worthy or "good" enough to receive the desired answer. The mixed results people have had at best with these approaches to God have further solidified the belief in a capricious often vengeful Deity who answers prayers, if at all, solely according to His whims.

Certainly, we experience genuine needs and heartfelt desires that impel us to seek a deeper connection with God. If we are not to approach our divine Source through reciting rote prayers, appeasing, bargaining or begging God for mercy, how then *are* we to pray? Is there a way to cultivate a more intimate and satisfying relationship with our heavenly Source, a method of praying in which we are always assured of an answer? New Thought holds the answers.

In the New Thought teachings, we do not subscribe to a harsh concept of the Deity; nor do we view prayer as an empty mechanical ritual or an exercise in religious gymnastics designed to sway an unforgiving God. Jesus stated his specific opposition to this type of prayer in his stern warning against "uttering vain repetitions as the heathen do" (MATT.6:7). He explained that if the answers to our prayers are not received it is not because of any unwillingness on God's part. Rather, it is because in some way we have not fulfilled the conditions for answered prayer. If we do not receive it is "because [we] ask amiss"(JAMES 4:3). Certainly, begging for Divine favor is asking amiss.

What then is the *right* way to pray? How can we be assured of peace in times of turmoil, comfort in our darkest hours and fulfillment of our souls' sincere desires? The New Thought teachings of metaphysical truth, with their direct derivation from the Bible, hold the key. In our study of New Thought we learn that the highest form of prayer is not to beseech a remote external Divinity for answers to our needs or resolution of our problems, (which is in essence an expression of the mistaken belief that we are separated from our spiritual Source) but rather to turn within to our inner sanctuary, described in Psalm 91:1 as "the secret place of the Most High," and to abide in this interior place, therein to know our Oneness with our Divine Source. Dwelling in this awareness, we come to know consciously that there is only One Presence and One Power, and that we live and move and have our being *in* it. This is what Jesus meant when he said "Men ought always to pray and not to faint" (LUKE 18:1).

As we bring our thoughts into harmonious alignment with Universal Mind, sometimes called the Christ-Mind, we begin to know the peace that Jesus spoke about, "the peace that passeth understanding" and every aspect of life becomes ordered. May Rowland, the long-time director of Unity's prayer ministry, expresses it thusly in her spiritual treatment entitled "Come Ye Apart Awhile":

> Through prayer, we put into action those higher laws which
> are innate in every man and each one of us becomes the
> conquering man.

Through daily prayer we become acquainted with the source
of spiritual strength and the tremendous reserves of power that
lie dormant within us are quickened into activity, with results
becoming tangible in every area of our lives. Note that entering
into the high place in consciousness – the holy chamber within
— and abiding there, is not the exclusive prerogative of the few;
it is an avenue open equally to all who seek it.

As implied above, in the mainstream Christian denominations
prayer is often a monologue in which the pray-er does all the
talking! He sends up (and God is usually thought of as "up
there", as we saw in the chapter on the nature of God) a laundry
list of petitions and requests. The notion of prayer as a two-way
conversation in which God also gets to speak does not seem
to enter into the picture. In New Thought we emphasize the
importance of inner attunement, of quieting the endless chatter
of the conscious mind and transcending the ceaseless torrent of
thoughts, by developing the art of focusing the awareness inwardly
for impressions and guidance from the higher Source. Present-
day spiritual author and teacher Iyanla Von Zant advocates
"listening for instruction rather than begging for direction." Joel
Goldsmith calls this state of receptivity "the listening ear" and
says that developing it is essential for receiving answers in prayer
(SIoS, pp.157-58).

Unity author Frances Foulks expresses the same emphasis on
the necessity of hearing in these words:

Spiritual deafness will cease when we really cross the threshold into the silence, for the inner ear will become alert to catch the message of the small, still voice...It may be some great message repeated that the Master spoke when among men bearing some new meaning and usefulness for you personally. It may be some individual message to comfort, to life, to strengthen, spoken to you when the veil is lifted and you pass beyond, into the holy of holies. Nevermore will you doubt the possibility of meeting God and talking with him in the secret place when once you have gone beyond the silence and seen him face to face, holding sweet communion with him in the garden of your soul (EF, P. 91).

The Bible endorses the New Thought practice of focusing the attention inwardly during times of prayer, even in the early writings of the Old Testament prophets and leaders. God is to be found not in the whirlwind, not in the fire, the prophet Jeremiah counsels the reader, "but in the *small, still voice*" (1KINGS19:12). The Old Testament leader, Samuel, caught the realization that our role in prayer is to *listen* inwardly and yield to the impartations received. He expresses his understanding in this way: "Speak Lord, for Thy servant heareth" (1SAM.3:10).

And David, concurring with Jeremiah and Samuel about the necessity of establishing a state of inner quietude as an essential precursor of answered prayer, writes in Psalm 46:10:"*Be still* and know that I am God." Stillness, then, is the first prerequisite to that experience of The Presence which is the ultimate goal of prayer. This "listening ear" must be intentionally and systematically cultivated, however, as our metaphysical authors advise. Though the Divine voice may not be experienced as audible sound, when it is received by the inner ear, it is unmistakable in Its Power and authority and we do well to heed Its directives.

What other conditions of answered prayer we are to cultivate? What attitudes of mind and heart are conducive to receiving answers? Let us examine the recommendations of metaphysical teachers and then see where we may find Biblical support for their counsel. To begin with, most New Thought practitioners emphasize the need for privacy in spiritual matters. Why is secrecy in spiritual practice a must? It is because there is a sound metaphysical principle at work here, a principle known to and taught by most New Thought teachers and it is this: If we talk indiscriminately about our inner life and those things for which we are treating, we dilute the power and efficacy of the prayer and often, the answer never quite materializes. Emmet Fox likens the act of discussing the issues of our soul to the photographic films of old which required a dark quiet place in which to develop fully. If they were exposed prematurely to the light of day, the resulting pictures were often incomplete, lacking clear images, or absent altogether.

We find more evidence in support of our metaphysical approach to prayer in the New Testament. In addition to Jesus' stern admonition against uttering rote prayers, he spoke out also against praying in a public manner to be seen of men, as the Pharisees were known to do. He taught that matters of the soul are sacrosanct and should be safeguarded with the utmost care. Like the cultivation of inner stillness, the observance of strict privacy in spiritual matters is a prerequisite to answered prayer. When we pray, he instructed us, we are to "enter into our prayer closet and therein to pray in secret," assuring us that "thy Father which seeth in secret shall reward [us] openly"(MATT. 6:6). Now Jesus did not mean that we are to enter a literal closet, of course, although it is always beneficial to set aside a room, an area of the home or a special place in nature that is conducive to prayer and meditation. Rather, he meant that we are to enter our inner chamber *in consciousness*, the private sanctuary deep within our soul where we discover and abide in the conscious awareness of our Oneness with God.

The Apostle Paul gave us other guidelines for effective prayer. In his Epistle to the Thessalonians (1 THESS.5:17), he adjures the reader to "pray without ceasing." This does not mean that we are to spend untold hours in religious rituals but rather that we are to live always in the awareness of communion with the Divine Presence within. Prayer is not to be reserved for special religious holidays or practiced sporadically when we are fearful, ill, or desperate but rather embraced *and applied* as a way of life. New Thought adherents honor this directive and try to live by it.

For metaphysical Christians, another important component of effective prayer is that we are to pray with the *expectation* of results, of receiving those things for which we have prayed. We are to *live in the answer*, as it were. The authors of the Bible tell us this throughout the Scriptures. "Wait my soul upon the lord", David writes, "for my *expectation* is from *him*" (PSA.62:5). There is to be no doubt, no equivocation, and no questioning on our part, just complete and unqualified faith that the desired outcome is even now forthcoming.

Throughout his ministry, Jesus reiterated the idea of complete and implicit trust in the Father's willingness to give his children the desires of their hearts. In the matter of prayer, he stated emphatically that we are to become as little children – in other words, open, yielded, and trusting, as we said in the section on entering the kingdom of heaven. We are to pray with a feeling of joyous anticipation and whole-hearted faith in the manifestation of the answer. In fact, as Thomas Troward reminds us, Jesus made our faith in the *certainty* of the answer the condition of receiving it (TLATW). "Whatsoever things ye desire, when ye pray, believe that ye receive them and ye shall have them" (Mark 11:24). It is in the *knowing* that the inner work is done, that the answer, already established in Being, takes form in the manifest realm. We can make these strong claims, Jesus asserted, because "it is [our] Father's good pleasure to give [us] the kingdom" (Luke 12:32). Our attitude of unwavering childlike trust and truly knowing our worthiness as sons and daughters of the Most High, paves the way for answers to flow forth from the unseen realm of ideation to the domain of tangible expression.

Cultivating the consciousness of oneness with the Source Jesus called 'the Father', and learning to *abide* in that awareness no matter what may be transpiring in the outer realms of life, is the highest form of prayer. Why is this so? It is because as we truly *know* our Oneness with our Source, the false sense of separation from God is transcended. The seeming boundary between our sense of a separate human identity and our Divine Source is dissolved. We are aware only of Oneness. There are no longer two, but One. In metaphysics we call this state of consciousness *realization* and it constitutes the true mystical union with the Divine which is the ultimate goal of prayer.

But how should we pray until we reach the state of conscious union with God that Joel Goldsmith and other mystics write of? How do we bridge the gap in consciousness between our so-called "normal" mental states and the state of ecstatic Oneness with God at the center of Being? The teachings of New Thought offer two useful interrelated techniques to quicken our experience of spiritual Oneness.

AFFIRMATION

The first of these is *affirmation*, an approach to prayer virtually unheard of within the tenets of traditional Christianity. In New Thought we place much emphasis upon affirmative prayer — positive statements of Absolute Truth — and the power of the spoken word. We learn that the spoken word is a mighty creative force because it sets in motion powerful currents of thought that stir the ethers and produce external results in accordance with their quality and essence. So rather than begging God for what we seem to lack, which is actually an expression of our lack of faith in the all-sufficiency of Spirit, we make powerful declarations that we already have or *are* those things which are desired, because in the greater Reality, this is the Truth!

Again, we can look to the Bible for sound instruction in the matter of prayer. We are told that we are to "decree a thing and it shall be established unto us," that our words "do not go forth void"; rather, they "accomplish that which we please and prosper in the thing whereunto we send them"(ISA.55:11). Since our words impress the very ethers with their vibrational frequency, they go forth charged with creative power that resonates with their particular quality and intent. Knowing this, we want to choose our words wisely in order to ensure that the desired results will be forthcoming.

For example, if we are feeling ill or weak, we might paraphrase Paul's instruction to the Ephesians in this affirmation: "I am strong in the Lord and in the power of His might"(Eph.6:10). If our bank account appears to be depleted we might make a strong decree such as the following: "I am a rich child of a beloved Father and it is His good pleasure to give me the kingdom of all Good." Or simply "God is my all-sufficiency in all things."

Affirmation is frequently used in conjunction with *denial*. Denial is that phase of prayer in which we rebuke, often verbally, the power of any negative condition to limit, bind, or defeat us. It is the *dissolving* activity of prayer in which we use the power of the spoken word to dismantle any negative thought-structures to which we have given credence or authority. When stating a denial, however, it is important to follow it immediately with an affirmative declaration of Absolute Truth, as in this sequence spoken by May Rowland:

I am not bound in personal consciousness. I am free
with the freedom of Spirit!

A cautionary note about affirmations: When using them it is important to keep them fresh and alive with feeling and not repeat them mechanically as a parrot would. With his typical incisive advice, Emmet Fox writes: "Those who work like a parrot inevitably make the parrot's demonstration – they remain in the cage!" (PTCT, p.177).

Spiritual Treatment

The second technique to quicken our experience of spiritual oneness is *spiritual treatment*, a series of bold, positive, usually vocalized, affirmations of spiritual Truth such as the foregoing, that comprise a form of prayer virtually unknown to mainstream Christians but used frequently by adherents of the New Thought philosophy. Treatment in the face of negative appearances, whether done for ourselves or another person, is a powerful way to alter negative appearances, and often brings about an instantaneous shift in, or complete dissolution of, the undesirable manifestation.

As we deny any and all negative conditions in the course of treatment we are following the dictum of Jesus Christ who counseled us not to judge "according to the appearance, but judge righteous judgment"(Jn.7:24). In treatment we recognize the unseen reality of Good as the Truth of our Being and remain undaunted and serene in the face of circumstances that would belie the goodness and almightiness of God.

It is important to end our spiritual treatment with an expression of thankfulness. Heartfelt gratitude unifies us in thought immediately with the Source of all Good, unlocking and unblocking obstructions in our consciousness and opening the floodgates of the soul to receive an unimpeded flow of abundant blessings.

A treatment for dissolving apparent sickness in the body and re-establishing the consciousness of wholeness, for example, might take a form similar to the following:

A SPIRITUAL TREATMENT FOR HEALTH

God is Life. God is Wholeness. God is Pure Being, the
Source of all Life.

God is the eternal Principle of Perfect well-being.

I am the beloved child of God and I am created in his
image and likeness.

I have all the attributes of God in the Truth of my being.

The Truth of my being is incorporated into every atom
and cell of my body temple.

Therefore, no dis-ease can outpicture here for God is the
only Presence and Power in my body.

Sickness has no claim on me!

The Truth of my Being shines through me now, blessing,
healing, purifying and restoring me.

I am the Perfect Life of God in expression and
I know this now.

I am renewed and restored on every level of my being.

Gods' healing activity is at work within me now
and I am healed.

I am a radiant being!

I express the Perfection of God in mind, soul, and body.

I rejoice in the Truth of Divine Healing as I claim my
complete and perfect healing NOW.

I thank God for the perfect demonstration of His healing
Love and Power in every aspect of my being.

And so it is.

Now that's prayer in action, the prayer that gets results!

CHAPTER 9

True Atonement

"I express perfect attunement — at-one-ment — with
all Divine Ideas."
— Rev. Adelaide Cotter, Unity minister

Our birth is but a sleep and a forgetting...
—William Wordsworth, *Ode: Intimations of Immortality*

For He is our peace, who hath made both one,
and hath broken down the middle wall
of partition between us (Eph. 2:14).

Adherents of the mainstream Christian denominations are
taught from their earliest days in Sunday School that Jesus Christ
re-established the Atonement between God and man broken by
Adam and Eve's 'fall' in the Garden of Eden. Jesus, it is believed,
brought about the reconciliation between a remote external God,
long displeased by the disobedience of His first children and the
unregenerate flock of humankind, by taking upon himself the
entire weight of human sin through his sacrificial death on the

Cross. In this singular act, he is said to have atoned *vicariously* for all the sins of mankind, past, present, and future. We should note, however, that if Jesus' death *had* in fact achieved atonement for all of humanity, the ills of mankind would no longer exist. As Charles Fillmore observed:

> Men have formed erroneous ideas about the Atonement…
> The Atonement as it has been understood by Christian people in the past has not taken sin, suffering, and death from the world; therefore, it must be that their understanding has fallen short of the Truth (MBD, P.79).

Jesus' proclamation that "I and my Father are One" (JN.10:30) has solidified in the minds of most God-fearing Christian folk the belief that Jesus and his Heavenly Father, are in fact, one and the same. They are correct to a point, but only if we remember that Jesus is speaking here, as he often does throughout the gospels, not as the man of Galilee but from the level of Christ awareness which *always* knows itself to be One with the Source of All, the source Jesus often refers to in the Scriptures as "my Father." It is not the individual Jesus who re-established man in right relationship to his Creator but rather, the work of the universal Christ Principle that indwelt him and indeed, dwells within us all. Here is where the process of reconciliation – atonement — takes place.

So clearly, the Atonement must have a much deeper meaning than that stated in Christian dogma. As with many of the other tenets of traditional Christianity, New Thought presents a more illumined understanding of the atonement process and its implications for the human spirit and for all of mankind. In *Stake Your Claim* Emmet Fox writes:

> ...not only are we and God one...but it is He who has
> made us one, and not ourselves as the result of hard work.
> We are One because that is the nature of being and He has
> made us that way (P.58).

We must bear in mind that atonement does not create a state of
unity between man and his divine Source that has never existed
previously. Atonement *re-establishes our conscious awareness* of that
unity which *is* now, and forever *has* been. Through the process
of atonement our souls begin to stir and awaken from the false
sense of separation from our Divine Source – the sleep of deep
amnesia into which, like Adam after his expulsion from Eden,
we have fallen – and we re-awaken to our *true* nature as sons and
daughters of the Most High, one with our Creator and indeed,
all creation. Kenneth Carey writes:

> In [our] natural state of creation, [we] have no sense of
> identity distinct from the Creator, except when [we] are
> engaged in a relationship...When... a relation-ship is not
> taking place, we float effortlessly in the potential of God.
> [We] are not annihilated, but all definitions of [us] are, and
> [we] are released from their restraining influence, allowed
> to expand into a state of love and perfection. (ST, P. 9)

Any feeling of estrangement from our Heavenly Father we may
have experienced comes from our own sense of a selfhood that
exists apart from God. This is the "wall" between ourselves and
God that the Apostle Paul describes in the verse from his Epistle
to the Ephesians cited at the beginning of this chapter, and it is
this partition – false sense of *a-part-ness*—that is "broken down"
– reconciled — by the work of the indwelling Christ.

Fillmore writes in the tract entitled *Jesus Christ's Atonement:*

> To comprehend the atonement requires a deeper insight
> into creative processes than the average man and the
> average woman have attained, not because they lack the
> ability, but because they have submerged their thinking
> power in a grosser thought stratum. Only those who study
> Being from the standpoint of pure mind can come into
> an understanding of the atonement and the part that Jesus
> played in opening the way for humanity to enter into the
> glory that was theirs before the world was.

We discern that the indwelling spirit of Truth, alone, "can reveal
the true meaning of Jesus Christ's mission and work" (MBD, p.79).
Even at first glance we see that the word 'atonement' itself can be
broken down into the three syllables, *at-one-ment.* This suggests
to us that the atonement is in truth, the at-*tune*-ment of our
individualized consciousness with the One Mind, Presence,
and Power. Therefore, it can be experienced by all who attune
themselves to the Christ within. The process of atonement is
indeed orchestrated by the Christ but it is the inner Christ, our
own higher consciousness of Oneness with the Source, that
does the work of reconciliation. The Atonement is a mighty
activity with far-reaching implications because it signifies the
permanent healing of the belief in two powers. It is a holy process
of reintegration, reunification if you will, that takes place deep
within the soul and it is available to us all at any time we make
the sacred commitment consciously to unify ourselves in mind
and heart with the indwelling Lord of our Being and function
from that awareness of Oneness.

Psychologist William James writes at length and in depth about the healing activity of reunification, detailing many case studies of personal examples in which a split or fragmented psyche became integrated and whole. He cites the example of Russian author Leo Tolstoy's own awakening from the Adamic sleep of duality to the experience of mystical union with the God-Presence:

> ...one day in early spring I was alone in the forest, lending my ear to its mysterious noises. I listened and my thought went back to what...it was always busy with—the quest of God. ...and again there arose in me glad aspirations toward life. Everything in me awoke and received a meaning. Why do I look farther? A voice within me asked. He is there, he without whom one cannot live. Well then! Live, seek God and there will be no life without him. After this, things cleared up within me and about me, and the life has never wholly died away (VRE, p. 157).

In New Thought we understand this direct apprehension of one's conscious Oneness with All-That-IS as a very sacred and intimate process of mystical union with God. We recognize Tolstoy's experience cited above as one of Atonement – the transcendent and permanent resolution of the belief in duality.

On the website of a spiritual group called The Temple of the Living Presence I came across the article excerpted below on the true selfhood of each of us that emerges when we transcend the belief in a separate selfhood and rediscover our true identity as sons and daughters of the Most High:

The Real You

Each of us is an individual manifestation of that Divine Flame of Life, having come from the Heart of God willingly and purposefully. Yes, the same God who made the whole macrocosm is focused within your own Individual I AM Presence. And within the fullness of that Presence is all that you desire, all that you require to fulfill your life. As you acknowledge this as the Truth of your Being, you begin to draw it forth.

There is so much more to life than the struggles and concerns customarily pre-occupying outer consciousness. It is possible to throw off those shackles of limitation that impose small-mindedness and leave you prey to forces that toss you about like pawns on a chessboard. You can strip away ignorance, blindness, superstition, and carelessness. For your True Reality is that, as a Firstborn Son or Daughter of God, you have the Power of your Mighty I AM Presence trembling on the cusp of your very own Heart.

Since that moment in Eternity known as "the beginning," the Perfect Blueprint of you has existed in the Mind of God. Life has continued for millions of years because the Eye of God and the Mind of God have steadfastly remained upon this Vision of the Divine you. Regardless of your inner struggles or outer appearances, this is the you your Presence recognizes and champions. And through conscious awareness, you can re-align your life and step into the Flame of Freedom that awaits you within the embrace of that Presence.

This is the eternal Self of us that has never been born and will never die. In our willingness to surrender the 'little' self and all that is associated with it, the perfect Self that has always existed in Divine Mind emerges and we are one with the One.

Joel Goldsmith writes of the permanent healing of the belief in two powers in all of his books and states that "conscious oneness with God constitutes [our] oneness with all spiritual being and with every spiritual idea or thing" (CUG,P.31). This merging of the human sense of self with the Divine, what he calls mystical or conscious union with God, is the ultimate goal of prayer. It is in fact what he terms "the new meaning of prayer." In *Beyond Thoughts and Words* he says that we are to approach prayer, not as supplication and entreaty to a remote God Who is separate from His creation, as discussed in the preceding chapter; we are to experience God as *communion* with Universal Being. He continues the same theme in *Practicing the Presence*:

> There is not God *and* you or I, there is only God, expressed, manifested as individual being...There is only one life, the Father's. We are outside of heaven with no hope of ever gaining entrance to it as long as we believe that we have a selfhood apart from God, a being separate and independent of God....all through the ages, duality has separated us from our good, but it is a *sense* of duality, not duality, because there is no duality. The secret of life is oneness...and Oneness is a state of being (P.56).

The author often uses a wonderful phrase: "'Tabernacle' with God." He means that we must know God in the sacred chamber of our innermost soul. Here, in the stillness of inward contemplation, the seeming boundary between our individual identity and God disappears and we merge in a sense of glorious Oneness. In this attunement of mind and heart to the Source, the sense of separation yields to At-One-Ment. We ask nothing; we simply rest in pure Being. We know God as our daily bread, the substance of our very life. We dwell consciously in the awareness that "in God we live and move and have our being." There is no worry about the future because we are completely centered in God as our all-sufficiency in all things. God not only lives IN us but It lives AS US. In one of the great paradoxes of spiritual Truth, Goldsmith writes, when we enter a state of non-power we then have access to the One Source of All-Power. Surrender, he claims, is the key to entering this state, which is grace.

The direct immediate experience of God's Grace is the highest form of prayer and constitutes *True Atonement*.

CHAPTER 10

The Power of Resurrection

I am the resurrection and the life (Jn. 11:25).

The Science of Mind takes seriously the dictum of being
recreated by the renewing of our mind. And not just our
minds, but our bodies and souls as well.

— Jean Houston, foreword to *The Science of Mind*

I am aware that every part of my body is continually being
replaced by new atoms, new life, in a perpetual
dance of resurrection.

— Richard JaFolla, former Director of Silent Unity

The physical raising of Jesus from the dead, celebrated by
Christians throughout the world at Easter, is one of the most sacred
and joyous holy days on the Christian Church calendar. There
is a quality in the human spirit that thrills to witness something
that has seemed dead being restored to life by miraculous means.
Each Spring as we see trees, shrubs and blades of grass that
have been brown and lifeless clothed anew with greenery by

a mysterious and wondrous process of renewal, our spirits are filled with joy and rightly so. We sense intuitively, however, that resurrection is more than an annual occurrence that takes place in Nature. The message of Spring calls to the life-impulse within us and we recognize instinctively that resurrection is an eternal process that happens not only in the natural world, but even more miraculously, within *us*.

For adherents of mainstream Christianity, however, The Resurrection was an isolated event that occurred once in the history of the world to a Divine being called Jesus Christ and solidified His claim to be the Son of God. Now The Resurrection may or may not have happened in the strict literal sense; probably this can never be authenticated or disproved. We have realized through a study of the New Thought teachings, however, that there is deeper meaning and profound personal significance to the events of Jesus' life; we have discerned that the historical occurrences are a metaphor for evolutionary processes always at work within *us*. We have evolved from learning "about" Jesus Christ as the only begotten Son of God who shed his blood to save us from our sins, to recognizing the Truth of our own being: that the Christ principle — of which the man Jesus was the fully realized embodiment — dwells within each one of us as our own inherent spiritual capacity to overcome.

It is vital in the instance of Jesus' resurrection from the dead, perhaps more than any other event in his life, that we fully comprehend the difference between his human personhood and his identity as the individualized expression of the Christ Principle within all of us. As the full implication of resurrection begins to take hold within our consciousness, we move away from viewing it as a singular historical event that may or may not have occurred thousands of years ago. Rather, we begin to comprehend and *celebrate* resurrection as a process that is going on within us *now* and at all times. We thrill to the realization that the resurrection of Jesus Christ represents the complete regeneration of the individual – our redemption from states of sin, sickness and death and restoration to our original estate of wholeness and perfection. As such, it has tremendous significance for our evolution as spiritual beings.

Charles Fillmore writes:

> The power of the resurrection is the Christ …the resurrection takes place in us every time we rise to Jesus' realization of the perpetual indwelling life that is connecting us with the unified consciousness we call the Father. A new flood of life comes to all who open their minds and their bodies to the living word of God (TRW, PP.169-170).

We understand that when Jesus spoke the words: "I AM the resurrection and the Life" (JOHN 11:25) he was speaking from the vantage point of the Christ Spirit within each of us. He was in effect declaring the Truth of Being, the truth of our own inherent divine potential. He was making the claim of *universal personal transformation*. Otherwise, he would not have said, *could* not have said, "He that believeth on me, the works that I do ye shall do also; and greater works than these shall he do" (JN. 14:12). This is a claim we can stand on.

Through his own "acting out" process of crucifixion and resurrection, Jesus demonstrated emphatically that there was a Principle at work here, an eternal principle that is valid and demonstrable for us all! This is why at another juncture, the Bible states that "Jesus Christ [is] the same yesterday, today, and forever" (HEB.13:8). The Principle of resurrection and the potential for its manifestation in the physical body hold true for all people, in all times, and in every situation. Renewal, healing, profound change, and revolutionary personal growth are possible for each of us because the seed idea of resurrection is encoded within the very atoms and cells of our being. This is why we can claim that the New Thought teachings with their emphasis on spiritual growth *and* physical regeneration derive directly from the words, teachings, and demonstration of Jesus and establish *metaphysical* Christianity as the unique inheritor of the Christ mantle.

Once we have gleaned even a rudimentary understanding of what this means, we begin to view the crucifixion of Jesus not as an experience of helpless martyrdom, nor the cross of Calvary as the ultimate symbol of suffering, humiliation, and sacrifice, but rather as supreme symbols of spiritual *victory*. We learn to approach personal times of severe testing — crucifixion experiences — with a growing awareness of the ever-present and victorious Christ Spirit within. We recognize that as we move through the trials of our own lives, all that is negative or limiting *within our own consciousness* can be "crossed out", succeeded by triumphant resurrection over any seeming challenge and culminating in our eventual ascension to higher levels of being.

In order for the life-transforming power of the Christ principle to work on our behalf, however, it must be *activated*, called forth from the realm of Divine potential to be utilized in the practical dilemmas of our daily lives. When faced with "crucifixion" experiences, the seemingly insurmountable challenges which confront all of us in the course of living — a frightening medical diagnosis, the unexpected termination of a primary source of income, the loss of a cherished loved one, the break-up of a significant relationship — any one of many overwhelming threats to life as we have known it, our initial response may be to feel as if we will never get through it, never again be the same, that we may as well throw in the towel right now.

How then do invoke the mighty redeeming activity of the Christ in us and mobilize its miracle-working power on our behalf? By putting into practice the New Thought teachings of pure spiritual Truth, we learn to move *through* these times of great testing — these dark nights of the soul — and emerge with greater clarity, strength and purpose. Eventually we are lifted — *resurrected* — out of personal darkness, in whatever form it may have assumed, into the light of greater understanding. Then, we are truly ready to live our lives from a higher vantage point, a more exalted level of our own being. This is *ascension*.

Now as we come to the end of this book, let us apply the idea of resurrection with singular focus and intention to one of the central themes of the New Thought philosophy, a theme not espoused and indeed, virtually unheard of, in the doctrines of mainstream Christianity: the *healing, restoration,* and *regeneration* of the physical body. Nowhere in traditional Christian dogma do we find any statement of the power of consciousness to order experience and seldom in the formal doctrines of Christianity do we find any mention of the power of constructive thought to heal, restore and regenerate the physical body. Quite the contrary, in fact. In many of the mainstream denominations, sickness is still thought to be either "the work of the devil", (who afflicts even the most undeserving of folks), or it is regarded as God's will. In the latter case, physical distress is actually esteemed and people are told to bear their afflictions stoically. Through pain and suffering, it is believed, they are identified with the agony of Jesus Christ on the Cross and therefore, assured of a place closer to the throne of God.

In New Thought we view physical illness in a far more enlightened way. We are in accord with contemporary scientists who tell us that the cells comprising the organs and tissues of our bodies are completely replaced many times over in the course of a lifetime. We note in observing our own bodies that cuts and bruises heal spontaneously without any conscious effort on our part, clear evidence of a regenerative activity always at work within us — the same principle of renewing Life that operates in Nature. We rejoice in the healing power that silently and efficiently orchestrates the myriad complex and intricate functions of our bodies to maintain us in wholeness and restore us when we have departed in thought from the perfect pattern.

So, unlike traditional Christian thought, healing figures very prominently in the tenets of metaphysical Christianity. It is in fact, central to our philosophy. New Thought is, and has been since its inception in the mid-nineteenth century, a healing philosophy. The ability of consciousness to recreate the body and restore it to its rightful pattern as the image and likeness of God is taught, embraced *and practiced* throughout the New Thought movement. In fact, the main New Thought groups — Unity, Religious Science (CSL), and Divine Science, like Christian Science a few decades earlier — came into being following the miraculous healings of their founders, individuals whose conditions were pronounced dire or even incurable by the medical practitioners of their day, solely through prayer and the right use of thought. On what basis did these individuals claim and manifest complete healing in bodies that were ravaged by disease? The answer is quite simple: they looked to the teachings of the Bible, specifically the example of Jesus Christ, discerned that there was a universal law at work and determined to claim its power for themselves.

Jesus was thoroughly acquainted with this mighty restorative power. He taught it, demonstrated it and lived it. No discussion of the legacy of Jesus Christ to the New Thought movement would be complete without an acknowledgment of the marvelous healing work that characterized his mission on earth. His prolific and unequivocal demonstrations of healing all manner of ailments and afflictions is a testament to the pervasiveness and indestructibility of the Life Principle and tangible evidence that healing is *always* the will of our Heavenly Father! To restate Jesus' declaration of the reason for his being on earth: "I am come that they may have *life* and that they might have it more abundantly" (Jn.10:10). The impetus behind his healing works was always to demonstrate that healing and regeneration were attainable by all who followed his example. He made no special claims to unique abilities for himself but, speaking as the Christ Principle indwelling each person, asserted that each of us has the potential to do the same regenerative works.

Let's look more closely at the Biblical basis for the New Thought pioneers' claims of healing and regeneration. The New Testament contains numerous references to the body as a temple. There are statements about the importance of recognizing it as the dwelling place of the spirit and the necessity of keeping it pure, undefiled and holy, as a prerequisite for resurrection. Just as a temple of masonry is constructed stone by stone until the edifice is whole and complete, so is the temple of the body built and rebuilt, right thought by right thought, until it is whole, complete, and *structurally sound*. So when the Bible speaks of rebuilding the temple, it is referring symbolically to the inherent capacity of the body for regeneration when supplied with the proper building materials in consciousness.

In Paul's Epistle to the Corinthians, he writes:

Know ye not that ye are the temple of God, and [that] the
Spirit of God dwelleth in you? (1COR.3:16)

If any man defile the temple of God, him shall God
destroy; for the temple of God is holy, which temple ye are
(1COR.3:17).

What? know ye not that your body is the temple of the
Holy Ghost [which is] in you, which ye have of God, and
ye are not your own? (1COR. 6:19)

....for ye are the temple of the living God (2COR.6:16).

In the four gospels, Jesus also makes numerous statements about
the purpose and function of the human body as a temple for the
indwelling spirit and he emphasizes the ability of the body to
be continuously renewed and restored. When the Jews question
Jesus about his assertion that he will be resurrected after death,
he responds that he is referring to his physicality:

Then said the Jews, Forty and six years was this temple
in building, and wilt thou rear it up in three days? (JN.2:20)

But he spake of the temple of his body (JN.2:21).

We have seen that regeneration is a universal healing activity that is at work tirelessly and ceaselessly, not only throughout Nature but within the very cells and atoms of our bodies. With the knowledge that healing and renewal are not only possible for us but already at work within us, how do we then use our spiritual faculties systematically to increase the regenerative activity? Some of the awesome powers we have at our command and guidelines to activate and accelerate these powers in the marvelous task of physical restoration are suggested below:

THE POWER OF RIGHT THOUGHT

Medical doctor and spiritual teacher Deepak Chopra contends that there is a principle of intelligence encoded within every atom and cell — a cosmic blueprint for wholeness — that knows how to restore the body to its original integrity when it is manifesting disease. The "patterns of intelligence we have built can be revised at any time," he declares in *Quantum Healing*, because "we recreate ourselves with every thought" (p. 155). "Wherever a thought goes, a molecule goes with it," he states, meaning that thought has the power to create physiological change *instantaneously*. Since the body is at all times a print-out of our consciousness, "the physical picture in 3-D" of what we are thinking, changes in one's habitual patterns of thought cause corresponding changes at the physical level (p.65).

That there is a silent universal intelligence continuously at work in the body, a supreme Mind that not only creates the physical form but renews and re-creates it when the blueprint becomes distorted, is what metaphysicians have always known and claimed. Many years before Deepak Chopra and other present-day spiritual teachers, Charles Fillmore said "We must get the mind-body connection." For those of us in New Thought, healing is not a matter of generating a cure from without, but rather lies in reconnecting ourselves *in consciousness* to the inherent perfection always underlying the apparent distortion.

We find Biblical support for the power of consciousness to alter bodily conditions in Jesus' question to his followers: "Which of you by taking thought can add one cubit unto his stature?" (MATT. 6:27) The preceding quote has been used to imply that it is impossible for mental processes to alter physical conditions. Alternatively, and in the context of the New Thought teachings, Jesus' question can be read as a challenge, an *invitation* to his listeners to demonstrate the power of *right thought* to effect discernible positive changes in the physical body.

THE POWER OF THE SPOKEN WORD

Metaphysicians have always known of the power of the spoken word to activate Substance for the purpose of eliciting a healing response in the body (and metaphysical author Florence Scovel Shinn devoted an entire book of the same name to the subject). In her own challenge of overcoming advanced tuberculosis, Unity's co-founder Myrtle Fillmore, a woman of great spiritual vision, used the power of faith-filled words to regenerate her body temple. Employing the Biblical axioms that claim "A merry heart doeth good like a medicine" (PROV.17:22) and "the joy of the Lord is [my] strength" (NEH.8:10), Mrs. Fillmore systematically praised and blessed her body for its perfect functioning. She was convinced that by approaching the Spirit with uplifted consciousness, most especially in the face of a healing challenge, and *vocally* calling forth the intelligence and perfection residing in each cell, she could activate a realization of her intrinsic wholeness, and her entire being — body, mind and spirit – would respond by bringing forth the perfect image that is held eternally in Divine Mind. In this way, she could resurrect her body from the experience of so-called incurable illness. In a chapter of her healing letters entitled *Understanding the Body* she writes:

> We need to use the vigorous life of Spirit to build up our body temple. Let us pour out upon our organism blessings of praise for the good work it is doing in establishing wholeness. Let us think of ourselves as already manifesting perfection in mind, soul, and body, and give thanks that Divine Order is now established (p.41).

And in a spiritual treatment entitled *Meditations on the Quest* Richard Jafolla, former director of Silent Unity, also uses the spoken technique with joy and enthusiasm to stimulate the healing life inherent within each cell of the body:

> I speak to the organs, tissues, and the cells of my body, praising and encouraging them with words and feelings of radiant life. I visualize their joy and eagerness to create health and life as they call forth the healing Presence!

Once again, we can find Biblical support for speaking life-giving words of Truth to evoke a healing response in a body that is out-picturing imperfection. Jesus knew and used powerful decrees to evoke the regenerative activity. In a well-known episode in his ministry, he is approached by a centurion who beseeches the Master to heal his servant, who is gravely ill at a distance:

> Lord, I am not worthy that thou shouldest come under my roof: but *speak the word only*, and my servant shall be healed (MATT.8:8).

> And Jesus said unto the centurion, Go thy way; and as thou hast believed, [so] be it done unto thee. And his servant was healed in the selfsame hour (MATT.8:13).

We note here that it was not necessary for Jesus to be physically present with the servant in order for the healing activity to take place. Because Spirit is not bound by time and space, the spoken word was sufficient to invoke the life-enhancing power and restore the servant to wholeness.

Surely, the most dramatic example of Jesus' demonstrating the mighty power of spoken words of Truth literally to restore life where death appears to hold sway, is the momentous instance in which he calls forth Lazarus, already dead for four days, from the tomb (JN. 11:43.):

> Jesus says to Mary and Martha "plainly, Lazarus is dead"
> (JN. 11:14).

> And when he had thus spoken, he cried with a loud voice,
> "Lazarus come forth" (JN. 11:43).

This example of the "living symbolism" which characterized Jesus' entire life, represents the power of the Universal Christ Principle of wholeness and Life to *call forth* the eternal presence of wholeness within, and resurrect us on every level, including the cells and atoms that comprise the holy temple we call the physical body.

THE POWER OF STILLNESS

Mighty works are wrought in stillness! Many years before doctors began to explore the possibility of a mind–body connection, metaphysicians like Joel Goldsmith treated hundreds of sick people solely through prayer. He affirmed the interrelation of spiritual healing and physical regeneration throughout his writings. In *The Art of Spiritual Healing* he expresses it this way:

> Healing is…finding ourselves in a spiritual peace…in inner peace. Resting in that peace, the body begins to show forth perfect, complete, health, youth, vitality and strength (ASH, P.130).

Like all metaphysicians, splendid early twentieth century Truth teacher, H.B. Jeffery, emphasized that healing was not a rare condition to be sought after with effort and struggle, but rather the normal and natural state of each one of us as spiritual beings. In *The Principles of Healing* he writes of the ease with which the restorative power works when the right inner climate of stillness, quiet *knowing*, and resting in the everlasting arms is established:

> Healing is the result of attainment and is really secondary to the work within ourselves…If we are wholly conscious of the Truth that God is spirit, and that [we are] the offspring of God – spiritual beings – if we *know* this to be so, we shall find that healing will be done as quietly and easily as warmth is manifest in a room when the radiator is charged with heat (P.45).

Jeffery goes on to say that sickness is *always* the result of a "disturbance in man's relationship with Spirit… a failure to know God as love and to know that we are the beloved offspring of the Supreme" (p.78). Losing the awareness of our divine heritage as sons and daughters of the Most High by entertaining states of discord, predisposes us to manifesting sickness in the body. Conversely, when we abide in the Secret Place of the Most High, as the Psalmist calls that place of *knowing* deep within our souls, we "touch the place of understanding …where the Heavenly Presence is felt." Jeffery states that with this practice, "a person might become a new creature, then and there" (p. 49).

We need to let go of the idea that *effort* must be involved in bringing about healing and recognize with Unity minister Elaine Decker in her meditation entitled *Bodily Healing* that "it is the Light, the Love, the Intelligence within us that does the work, and we can relax and let healing and wholeness take place." Our only responsibility in the matter of bodily regeneration is to turn within, make conscious connection with our God-Source, and let IT do its perfect work. Thus, our work is always within our own consciousness for it is here in the domain of thought that we have full autonomy. We are to work consistently, steadfastly, and unceasingly, however, if we would see results.

The Apostle Paul adjures us to "have this mind that was in Christ Jesus" for it is the Christ Mind, the *undivided* mind, that ever beholds us in our original state of Divine perfection and glory. We have the capacity to align ourselves in consciousness with the Christ Mind for the purpose of healing.

Healing encompasses far more than the mere reduction of physical symptoms, however. In the New Testament Book of James we read "Let patience have [its] perfect work, that ye may be perfect and entire, wanting nothing" (JAM.1:4). Real healing is always the healing of the whole person – body, mind and spirit – and it always takes place from the inside out. Underlying causes in the mental realm are dissolved first; then the outer envelope of the body radiates the inner splendor that has been obscured by the overlay of false beliefs and unenlightened thinking.

Keeping in mind the living symbolism of the Master's life, we find in the story of Jesus' resurrection from the tomb, a metaphor for our own emergence from the sarcophagus of fear, insecurity and disease into the light of a new consciousness of health and life. At a Unity retreat I attended many years ago, minister Wilma Powell spoke these comforting and illuminating words about resurrection:

> In the darkness of every human experience, there is a Light
> that far outshines the darkness. Remember that the tomb
> of Jesus was a focal point of light.

In the stillness of deep prayer, to which we repair when it may seem as if there is no hope, the magnificent work of renewal and restoration is done within us and we emerge as resurrected beings, entering into a new dimension of experience.

THE POWER OF THE SPIRIT

As we have said, in New Thought we recognize that the physical body is a temple in which the eternal spirit dwells; as such, it contains the potential for complete restoration. Examples abound of individuals who have demonstrated the Reality of total bodily healing. A case in point is that of one of New Thought's great pioneers: Malinda Cramer. Mrs. Cramer, beset with long-standing health problems that did not respond to the curative measures of her day, experienced a profound spiritual awareness that resulted in her complete healing and inspired her to co-found Divine Science with Nona Brooks, who had experienced her own dramatic healing from a near-fatal throat infection. Cramer records her journey from sickness into health in the following excerpt from her magazine *Harmony*:

> Is there any way out of these conditions? Is there any power in the vast universe that can heal me? The immediate and all-convincing response was…an intuitive response by the life-giving spirit which penetrated the body through and through…which illumined and vivified every atom with newness of life. From the depths of Divine perception and understanding, I was caused to know…that if I got well it would be by the power of the Infinite Spirit (VOL.7, NO.1, OCT. 1894).

In like manner, Myrtle Fillmore, in the course of her own healing from tuberculosis, realized the essentially spiritual nature of the body and its inherent capacity for eternal renewal. In a flash of clarity, Myrtle suddenly knew that God was her Father and therefore, so-called hereditary sickness could make no claim upon her. She shares her revelation in these words:

> The physical claims that had been (of) such a serious nature faded away before the dawning of this new consciousness, and I found that my body temple had been literally transformed by the renewing of my mind.

And in *Spiritual Control of the Body*, she writes:

> A thing is no less spiritual because it has taken on form and weight and color...Evidently, the individual soul has felt the need of such an earth home as the body temple...We are convinced that the regular appropriation of certain life elements is required to maintain the body at a certain rate of vibration...which we know as health, and endurance and ability to transmute thought into action...
>
> When we can sustain the body in health and activity and radiance indefinitely, we shall have gained a better understanding of the true purpose of life and will be ready to enter upon a mode of living that may free us from the observance of laws that we may term "physical" (PP.74-75).

Many contemporary spiritual authors have recognized the positive effects that spiritual work has on the physical organism. Eckhart Tolle writes in *The Power of Now* that spiritual awareness has profound regenerative benefits for the human body. First, there is a significant slowing down of the aging process because the accelerated frequency of higher states of spiritual consciousness makes the body's molecular structure less dense and therefore, more vibrantly alive. Released from the burden of "psychological time" (harboring regrets about the past and anxiety about the future), the body is free to renew itself continuously as it was designed to do (PP.122-123).

Secondly, the immune system is greatly strengthened and its resistance to disease maximized. Tolle says that every cell "awakens and rejoices" in the awareness of regeneration (P.123). He also comments that the "psychic immune system" is enhanced, as well (p.124). By this he means that the electromagnetic field, the "aura" surrounding the physical body, is fortified and rendered impervious to onslaughts of negative energy from without. "Inner body awareness", as he terms it (p.115), really means that we are abiding in conscious realization of Oneness with our Source. It is our realization of Oneness, as we said in the chapter on True Atonement, that allows regeneration to take place.

THE POWER OF FAITH

We saw in the chapter on prayer that faith in the certainty of fulfillment is our assurance of answered prayer. The thought of faith "molds the undifferentiated Substance," Ernest Holmes writes, and "brings into manifestation the thing that was fashioned in the mind" (SOM, PP.156-57). As in every other area of life, if we would experience God's resurrecting power in our bodies, we must be convinced "that under Divine Law, all things are possible if we only believe and work in conformity with the principles of that Law" (p.162). Holmes goes on to say:

> Because we fail to realize that Principle is not bound by precedent, we limit our faith to that which has already been accomplished and few "miracles" result. When, through intuition, faith finds its proper place under Divine Law, there are no limitations, and what are called *miraculous* results follow (SOM, P. 162).

We have said in various ways throughout this book that we are bound only by the parameters of our consciousness. Those who have great faith, Holmes asserts, have great power, because when there is no ceiling to our faith, there is no limit to what is possible to us. When we can accept the notion of physical resurrection at a very deep level of our being as truly possible for us, the body will follow suit and bring it forth into manifestation.

In numerous instances of instantaneous healing in the Bible, Jesus tells the afflicted person, "Thy *faith* hath made thee whole." One such case is that of blind Bartimaeus, begging by the side of the road, whose verbal expression of implicit faith in Jesus' abilities is sufficient to instantly restore his sight. Another notable example is the instance in which Jesus is approached by a woman in need of healing:

> And, behold, a woman, who was diseased with an issue of blood for twelve years, came behind *him*, and touched the hem of his garment:
>
> For she said within herself, *If I may but touch his garment, I shall be whole.*
>
> But Jesus turned him about, and when he saw her, he said, "Daughter, be of good comfort; thy faith hath made thee whole." And the woman was made whole from that hour (MATT. 9:20-22).

In our metaphysical understanding of the events in Jesus life, we recognize that the woman's actions in touching Jesus' garment symbolize the Truth that even a superficial or fleeting contact with the living Christ is sufficient to activate *instantly* Its resurrecting power.

THE POWER OF FORGIVING LOVE

Of all the spiritual components required for total healing –
body, mind and spirit, forgiveness is the most direct path to
permanent freedom from sickness and the most powerful path
to regeneration of the body. This is why it has always been
emphasized so strongly by spiritual teachers, and in recent years,
psychologists and physicians, as well. Jerry Jampolsky writes in
the introduction to *Forgiveness*:

> We now know that lack of forgiveness—that is, clinging to
> anger, fear or pain – does have a measurable impact on our
> bodies. These create tensions that affect the physiological
> systems that we are dependent on for health. They affect
> the circulation of blood in our bodies. They affect the
> efficiency of our immune systems. They put stress on our
> hearts, on our brains, and on virtually every organ in our
> bodies. Lack of forgiveness is indeed a health factor.

In a treatise written many years ago entitled "A Sure
Remedy", Charles Fillmore says that forgiveness is a certain
cure for all of the problems of individuals and the world; he
recommends setting aside a half-hour each day expressly for the
purpose of forgiving individuals and situations that have caused
us unrest. Likewise, in a marvelous spiritual treatment called
"The Golden Gate" Emmet Fox affirms the miracle-working
power of forgiving love:

> There is no difficulty that enough love will not conquer;
>
> No disease that enough love will not heal;
>
> No door that enough love will not open,

No gulf that enough love will not bridge.

No wall that enough love will not throw down,

No sin that enough love will not redeem.

It makes no difference how deeply seated may be the trouble,

How hopeless the outlook,

How muddled the tangle,

How great the mistake.

A sufficient realization of love will dissolve it all.

If only you could love enough you would be the happiest and most powerful being in the world.

Pray for the understanding of divine love and meditate upon it daily.

It is the fulfilling of the law. It covers a multitude of sins.

Love is absolutely invincible" (PTCT, p. 267).

This is the unconditional love that is sufficient to redeem us from the tomb of darkened thought, the forgiving love that sets us free and completely renews, restores and resurrects the body temple.

As willing as we may be to forgive others, though, we often have difficulty in including ourselves! If we are to rise up in newness of life, however, we must extend the idea of forgiveness to the *self*. Ernest Holmes writes:

It is a blessed day when we are fully able to embrace the Truth of our status as children of our heavenly Father, eternally beloved and precious in His sight. When the magnitude and magnificence of this realization dawns within our consciousness, we will at last be able to let *ourselves* off the hook of self-blame and the fear of future damnation (SOM).

In the meantime, since God, as Law, can only do for us what He can do *through* us, if we would be forgiven and set free to realize our Divine destiny we must fulfill our part of the bargain, which is to release any grievance or animosity we have held toward another. Then the Law can work unimpeded on our behalf to bring us the desires of our hearts and restore our bodies to the perfect pattern of wholeness in which we were created.

Jesus taught and demonstrated the resurrecting power of forgiveness throughout his three-year earthly ministry. One of many instances of miraculous healings that came about directly as the result of forgiveness is found in the Gospel of Mark where the author recounts the story of Jesus' healing the palsied man:

And they come unto him, bringing one sick of the palsy, which was borne of four.

And when they could not come nigh unto him for the press, they uncovered the roof where he was: and when they had broken it up, they let down the bed wherein the sick of the palsy lay.

When Jesus saw their faith, he said unto the sick of the palsy, Son, thy sins be forgiven thee (MARK 2:3-5).

...whether is it easier to say to the sick of the palsy, *Thy* sins be forgiven thee; or to say, Arise, and take up thy bed, and walk?

But that ye may know that the Son of man hath power on earth to forgive sins, (he saith to the sick of the palsy,) I say unto thee, Arise, and take up thy bed, and go thy way into thine house.

And immediately he arose, took up the bed, and went forth before them all; insomuch that they were all amazed, and glorified God, saying, We never saw it on this fashion (MARK 2:9-12).

As the Master speaks the comforting words of compassion and forgiveness, the man's sense of self-condemnation and judgment is lifted, *allowing him to receive* Jesus' words of healing power and authority. The physical manifestation of infirmity departs instantaneously, and the young man obeys the command to rise, take up his bed and walk. Metaphysically interpreted, as the Universal Christ dissolves the underlying cause of the man's sickness, the corresponding effect is his restoration – *resurrection* — to complete wholeness.

The supreme demonstration of the power of forgiveness to restore life is of course Jesus' monumental triumph over death, an overcoming so magnificent in its implications for us both individually and collectively as a species that we do well to heed the tremendous lesson it contains. In Jesus' final hours on earth in the Garden of Gethsemane, even as he is experiencing the betrayal of those closest to him, he utters a statement of forgiveness and compassion so profound and heartfelt that it is difficult for the human self of us to encompass it:

Forgive them, Father, for they know not what they do.

(LUKE 23:34)

In this sublime recognition that there is no sin but ignorance, Jesus sets the stage for his victory over death.

With spiritual insight, we recognize that in this supreme gesture of unconditional love, Jesus illustrates for us the direct cause and effect relationship between forgiveness and resurrection. Through the Christ indwelling, as *we* truly forgive and let go of even the most painful experiences of injustice and the cruelest of betrayals, we experience complete liberation, freedom from all things of the earth and we are raised up into new levels of being. We can claim with the Master: "Lo, I have overcome the world." We recognize that all the injuries of body, mind or spirit were but "wounds to the mortal" aspect, as my father called them, affronts to the human sense of us that still believes we are separate. We know unequivocally that the Truth of our nature – which is that we are eternal spiritual beings — remains always whole, intact and inviolate. This is what Jesus means when, speaking as the Christ, he gives us this assurance:

> And I, if I be lifted up from the earth, will draw all [men] unto me (JN. 12:32).

Understanding the spiritual significance of Jesus' promise to uplift the entire consciousness of humanity, early New Thought pioneer, Emma Curtis Hopkins, also discerned the tremendous physical implications of Jesus' statement. In a declaration quite shocking for the time in which she issued it, Hopkins went so far as to insist upon the potential human ability to overcome death through the ongoing regeneration of the physical body. "Do not stop short of expecting to obey this last command of the risen Christ," she exhorted her students, a pronouncement that would profoundly influence the spiritual teachers who succeeded her, such as Charles and Myrtle Fillmore (EMK, p.74).

Mr. Fillmore believed that when Jesus uttered the words above, he was speaking not only as the indwelling Christ Principle perpetually uplifting us in consciousness *individually* but also disclosing that he, the physical being *Jesus*, was the template for all of humankind, the "first fruits of a new race of man," the forerunner of the next stage of human evolution. As our "Wayshower in Regeneration", Jesus through his own resurrection and ascension, modeled for us what *we* someday will do and become. Fillmore was convinced that those things which are beyond our present understanding to demonstrate and are therefore, deemed miraculous – such as the resurrection of the body — will in time be done easily and effortlessly by the human race. He goes on to say:

> [Truth students] are in all ways building up the perfect body-idea, transforming flesh corruptible into spirit incorruptible. Thus, they are following Jesus in the regeneration. When they have renewed every organ and every part, both within and without, and put away all evidences of old age, the world at large will begin to accept their claims as true: that the destiny of all men is to transform the body of flesh into a body of Spirit and thus immortalize it…Then resurrection will be part of our spiritual evolution and then we shall know *experientially* what Jesus meant by his death and resurrection (MJ, p.174 AND p.175).

So we see that the intrinsic desire of all humankind for Life eternal and the information we need in order to experience it is "encoded in the structural makeup of every cell in [our] body," as

Kenneth Carey tells us (ST, p.52). Since we know as metaphysicians that desire contains within it the seeds of its own fulfillment, we embrace the Truth that resurrection *will* become our actual experience, our ultimate Divine destiny as we continue to evolve, both individually and as a species. Carey refers to the shift that is already taking place in our fundamental sense of identity, declaring that we are coming to realize we are not the bodies we inhabit but rather "the force of animation itself" (p.53):

> You are not your body. You are not your thoughts. You are not what you feel, not your experience, or your role. You are the Spirit of Life itself, dancing in the clay, delighting in the glorious experience of incarnation, exploring the realms of matter, blessing the Earth, and all therein (ST, p.53).

That the human race is undergoing an evolutionary process which heralds the spiritualization of the physical body is becoming increasingly clear. New Thought practitioners and teachers, in particular, are aware of the shift that is taking place, a quantum shift in our understanding of who and what we really are as spiritual beings, and they are expressing this insight in their classes, workshops and books. May Rowland says in her *Come Ye Apart Awhile* meditation:

> The body is composed of trillions of atoms and at the center of every atom is light. We are commencing to realize that we are not mass and material but that we are essentially spiritual substance, Light and Intelligence.

And in *Meditations on the Quest* Richard JaFolla speaks of the holy activity within us, always moving us toward renewed health and stronger life:

All of the fresh new atoms are teeming with possibility and I make the commitment to provide only positive life-affirming thought patterns as a mold with which to nurture these atoms My [heartfelt] desire to be whole now turns into an expectation [that] pervades my entire existence.

It makes its way to a level beyond the tissues, beyond the cells, and even beyond the atoms, a level touched and known only in the silent empty spaces beyond all physical matter.

A new…awareness of the Life-force, the spirit of You within me, [provides] me with what I so ardently expect at the deepest level, your Life in me. This new awareness alone brings about new faith, a new pattern, and my physical body has no other option than to follow it into wholeness.

Your powerful healing Presence touches every atom of my being, calling forth a radiant wholeness and I AM HEALED!

There are veiled references to the potential experience of universal bodily resurrection in the Bible. The Apostle Paul is referring to our imminent collective transformation when he prophesied over two thousand years ago that "in a moment, in the twinkling of an eye, we shall [all] be changed" (1 COR.15:52). So we are on the brink of a spiritual awakening unparalleled in the history of humankind – the collective shift from ego to Presence, from separate selfhood to Universal Christhood and it is taking place now. The implications of Paul's statement and Jesus' proclamation that we would all be lifted up are *huge*, nothing short of revolutionary, because these pronouncements mean that *solely* by taking thought, we can change the prevailing vibrational frequency of our bodies, and thereby alter the very structure of reality as we know it. As we build the temple of a new consciousness thought by thought, we move from a theoretical understanding of metaphysics to knowing the Truth of Being *experientially.*

In completing this endeavor, I would like to cite Ernest Holmes' magnificent passage from a section of *The Science of Mind* entitled *The Triumphant Christ*:

> The Christ knows that his individuality is indestructible; that He is an eternal being, living forever in the bosom of the Father. The Christ triumphs over death and the grave, breaking through the tomb of human limitation into the dawn of eternal expansion. The Christ rises from the ashes of human hopes, pointing the way to a greater realization of life.
>
> THE CHRIST IS ALWAYS TRIUMPHANT, IS EVER A VICTOR, IS NEVER DEFEATED, NEEDS NO CHAMPION! The Christ places His hand in the outstretched hand and walks unafraid through life.
>
> We are never without a witness of the eternal, and in our greatest moments − in those flash-like visions of mystic grandeur − we know that we are made of eternal stuff, fashioned after a Divine Pattern (PP. 369-70).

This is and always has been our own Divine destiny, awaiting only our grand and glorious awakening!

Bibliography

Braden, Charles S. *Spirits in Rebellion.* Southern Methodist University Press: Dallas, 1963.

Butterworth, Eric. *Discover the Power within You.* Harper Brothers, publishers: New York, 1968.

Carey, Kenneth. *The Starseed Transmissions.* Uni Sun publishing: Kansas City, MO, 1982.

Emerson, Ralph Waldo. *Emerson's Essays,* with introduction by Irwin Edman. Harper and Row, publishers: New York, 1926.

Fillmore, Charles and Cora. *Teach Us to Pray.* Unity School of Christianity: Lee's Summit, MO, 1941.

Fillmore, Charles. *Mysteries of John.* Unity Books: Unity Village, MO, 1997.

Fillmore, Charles. *The Revealing Word.* Unity School of Christianity: Lee's Summit, MO, 1931.

Foulks, Frances W. *Effectual Prayer.* Unity School of Christianity: Lee's Summit, Mo, 1939.

Fox, Emmet. *Alter Your Life.* Harper and Row, publishers: New York, Evanston and London, 1931.

Fox, Emmet. *Find and Use Your Inner Power.* Harper and Brothers: New York and London, 1937.

Fox, Emmet. *Power through Constructive Thinking.* HarperSanFrancisco, *a division of* HarperCollins *publishers*, 1932.

Fox, Emmet. *Stake Your Claim.* Harper and Row: New York, NY, 1952.

Goldsmith, Joel S. *Beyond Thoughts and Words.* Lorraine Sinkler, ed. Acropolis Books, publishers: Atlanta, 1998.

Goldsmith, Joel S. *Conscious Union with God.* The Citadel Press: Secaucus, NJ, 1980.

Goldsmith, Joel S. *Spiritual Interpretation of Scripture.* DeVorss & Co., *publishers*, 1947.

Goldsmith, Joel S. *The Thunder of Silence.* Harper and Row: New York, 1961.

Holmes, Ernest. *The Science of Mind.* Jeremy P. Tarcher/Putnam of Penguin Putnam, Inc: New York, 1998.

James, William. *The Varieties of Religious Experience.* Megalodon Entertainment LLC on the web:, 2008, orig. published 1902.

Jeffery, H.B. *The Principles of Healing*. Ruth Laighton, *publisher.* Cambridge, 1929.

Kupferle, Mary. *God Never Fails.* Unity School of Christianity: Lee's Summit, MO,1959.

Metaphysical Bible Dictionary. Unity School of Christianity: Lee's Summit, MO, 1962.

Stubbs, Tony. *An Ascension Handbook*. World Tree Press. Lithia Springs, GA, 2009.

Tolle, Eckhart. *A New Earth*. A Plume Book. New York, New York, 2006.

Tolle, Eckhart. *The Power of Now.* Namaste Publishing and New World Library: Novato, CA, 1999.

Troward, Thomas. *The Dore Lectures on Mental Science.* Dodd, Mead and Company: New York, 1909.

Troward, Thomas. *The Edinburgh Lectures on Mental Science.* Dodd, Mead and Company: New York, 1909.

Troward, Thomas. *The Hidden Power*. WLC Books, 1921.

Troward, Thomas. *The Law and the Word.* DeVorss Publications, Camarillo, 2007.

Troward, Thomas. *Bible Mystery and Bible Meaning*. Kessenger Publications.

Whitney, Frank B. *Mightier than Circumstance.* Unity School of Christianity. Lee's Summit, Mo, 1935.

The Holy Bible {containing the Old and New Testaments} King James Version. The New World Publishing Company, Cleveland and New York.